A Note on Measures and Portions

All recipes in this book are designed to serve six persons. Each recipe has been tested using the measures originally given us by the chefs. Four of them used liquid or weight measures, and we made our tests accordingly in order to keep our recipes as close as possible to the originals.

Weight measurements can easily be made on a small kitchen scale, but for the convenience of those who may not have one we have listed below a brief table of common conversions.

S. G. and B. F.

GENERAL CONVERSIONS:

a pinch = $^1/_8$ teaspoon   4 tablespoons = $^1/_4$ cup
3 teaspoons = 1 tablespoon   2 cups = 1 pint
2 tablespoons = 1 ounce   2 pints = 1 quart
               1 pound = 16 ounces = 500 grams

BUTTER:
1 stick = $^1/_4$ pound = $^1/_2$ cup = 115 grams = 8 tablespoons
FLOUR:
1 cup = 5 ounces = 140 grams
1 tablespoon = $^1/_4$ ounce
SUGAR:
1 tablespoon = $^1/_2$ ounce = 15 grams
1 cup = 7 ounces = 200 grams
2 cups = $13^1/_2$ ounces = 400 grams

Dining Out & Dining In
Memorable Menus and Recipes
from
Washington's Finest Restaurants
Sheila Geoghegan and Bonnie Fitzpatrick
Foreword by James J. Kilpatrick

EPM Publications, Inc.
McLean, Virginia

Library of Congress Cataloging in Publication Data

Geoghegan, Sheila.
  Dining out & dining in.
    1. Cookery, International. 2. Menus. 3. Restaurants, lunch rooms,
etc.—Washington metropolitan area. I. Fitzpatrick, Bonnie. II. Title.
TX725.A1G355   641.5   81-200
ISBN 0-914440-47-0   AACR2

EPM Publications, Inc.
1003 Turkey Run Road, McLean, Virginia 22101

Book Design by Don Sheldon
Illustrations and cover by Jack Long
Production Consultant, Irv Garfield

FOREWORD

Forty years ago, when I first visited Washington, Roosevelt was in the White House, Cactus Jack Garner was presiding over the Senate, Sam Rayburn was Speaker of the House, and Harlan Stone was about to succeed Charles Evans Hughes as Chief Justice. It seems a long time ago. I was then a young Virginia newspaperman, and I hungered for assignments that would take me to the nation's capital. Then as now, Washington was an exciting city; it was more than the capital of the United States: It was the capital of the free world, and it had most of the attributes we associate with such capitals as London, Paris and Rome—embassies and limousines, and a constant going-and-coming of distinguished guests.

But, alas, Washington in those years was in many ways a provincial city also. It had the Smithsonian and the National Gallery, but no other museums of consequence. Its symphony was second rate, its theater season limited. And to get to the point, its restaurants, with few exceptions, were nothing to write home about. There were two or three good seafood houses, and there was the venerable Harvey's. Several of the fine hotels—the Mayflower, the Hay-Adams, the Shoreham—offered touches of elegance and haute cuisine, but no one ever thought of Washington as one thinks of New Orleans and New York, as cities in which one does not eat but rather dines.

The picture is astonishingly different now. The great restaurants of Washington can hold their own with the great restaurants of the world. Where once we had a choice of French or American dishes only, with maybe a good plate of manicotti at the Roma, today one finds menus of international scope. Washington has become a great city in which to go out to dinner.

Sheila Geoghegan and Bonnie Fitzpatrick discovered these happy aspects of our capital in the happiest possible way: They were forever being taken out to dinner by the various beaux who sought their company, and they made a point of trying different restaurants all the time. I should add, so that you may get to know them, that both young ladies are positive corkers. Sheila is short and Bonnie tall. They are both of Irish descent. And they both are marvelous cooks.

Together they conceived this cookbook. Dining out, they had learned, could be delightful. How about dining in? If the leading chefs would make available their recipes for an ideal dinner, maybe the dishes could be replicated in their own kitchens. So Bonnie and Sheila embarked upon a labor of love and gastronomy. They made up their own list of the restaurants they had especially enjoyed, and they went calling on the proprietors and the chefs.

The task proved more difficult than they had imagined at the outset. Some of the restaurant owners dragged their feet. A few chefs got temperamental. Two of the restaurants—Paul Young's, across from the Mayflower, and the legendary Duke Zeibert's, a block away on L Street—closed their doors. The most cooperative chefs had a way of writing out their menus with Gallic abandon—a soupspoon of this, a dash of that, a bouquet of something else. Sheila and Bonnie translated the recipes into dinners for six, and they tested every one. Their own dinner parties gained a spreading reputation—no double entendre is intended—among the young people of Washington and Rappahannock County. Some of us avuncular oldsters were invited to share the experiments. Yes, there were failures. One spectacular dessert proved a spectacular disaster and had to be abandoned. A pâté proved more trouble than it was worth. A few recipes called for ingredients so exotic that only the individual chefs knew where to find them. But after a year's appetizing labor, they were done.

The perfect dinners that follow were chosen by the great chefs themselves. Sheila and Bonnie chose the restaurants; no one paid to be included. The two compilers of this work hope that visitors to Washington—and local residents as well—will find as much pleasure as they found in first dining out, and then dining in. Bon appetit!

September 1980   JAMES J. KILPATRICK

AUX BEAUX CHAMPS

2800 Pennsylvania Avenue, N.W. · Washington, D.C. · (202) 342-0444

For romantic dining in unsurpassed surroundings, head for the Four Seasons Hotel at the edge of Georgetown, and descend the elegant staircase to Aux Beaux Champs.

Once inside you will be graciously escorted to your table. The tempting menu will make selection difficult. Try deciding from Medallions of Veal in a Creamy Tarragon Sauce, Poached Salmon with Red Caviar, Red Spanish Shrimp in Meaux Mustard Sauce or Chicken in Calvados Sauce. Whatever you choose, you will be delightfully surprised to learn that at last a hotel has been able to surpass the reputation of "hotel food."

The four-course menu that follows would provide a lovely evening for your guests at a black-tie dinner in your home.

The Duck Pâté with Rhubarb Compote is rich, full of flavor and moist. The Cream of Bay Scallops and Artichoke is an elegant and unusual appetizer.

The highlight of your dinner party will be the Carre d'Agneau Elizabeth—boned rack of lamb, with spinach and mushroom purée, baked in puffed pastry and served with Madeira sauce. Yes, so superb an entrée takes several hours to prepare, but it can be made in advance and it justifies the trouble. The watercress and celeriac purée offers a welcome change from the everyday vegetable.

Lemon Japonais with Strawberry Purée are light and outrageously good. And of course when you serve the coffee, don't forget some chocolate truffles!

Aux Beaux Champs

Freemark Abbey
Chardonnay 1978

La Terrine de Canard et Foie Gras
au Compote de Rhubarb
(Terrine of Duck and Foie Gras
with Rhubarb Compote)

Le Velouté des Petoncles et Arti-
chauts
(Cream of Bay Scallops and Artichokes)

Pommard "Clos de la
Commarine" 1971

Le Carre d'Agneau Elizabeth
(Rack of Lamb Elizabeth)

Les Deux Purées de Celeri et
Cresson
(Purées of Celeriac and Water-
cress)

Schramsberg "Blanc et
Noir" 1975

Le Japonais au Citron au Coulis
des Fraises
(Lemon Japonais with Strawberry
Purée)

Le Café
(Coffee)

Les Truffles au Chocolat
(Chocolate Truffles)

Terrine of Duck and Foie Gras with Rhubarb Compote

> 4 duck breast halves from two 4–5 pound ducks
> 2 ounces port wine
> salt and pepper
> rosemary and thyme
> 1 ounce unsalted butter
> 3 ounces puréed leeks confit
> 6 ounces foie gras (goose liver)
> 3 ounces puréed shallots confit
> 6 ounces reduced duck stock (see below)

Remove the breasts from the ducks, discarding skin and fat. Marinate in port wine. After four hours remove breasts and reserve marinade for later use.

In a large frying pan, sauté the ducks in butter, seasoning well with salt, pepper, rosemary and thyme. Remove breasts from the pan while still pink. Place two of the breasts in the bottom of a terrine. Sprinkle with a layer of confit of leeks (leeks sautéed in butter for 15 minutes or until tight; then puréed) and spread on a layer of foie gras (3 ounces). Pour on $^1/_2$ of the port marinade.

Place the remaining two breasts on top of the foie gras. Sprinkle with a layer of confit of shallots (3 ounces) and spread on a layer of the remaining foie gras (3 ounces). Pour on the remaining marinade. Add $^1/_2$ the reduced duck stock and apply pressure to compress the terrine. Let settle until the stock gels. Cover with the remaining duck stock. Refrigerate for one day before serving.
Note: The terrine has to be unmolded carefully. It is very delicate.

Duck Stock

Take the carcasses and legs of the two ducks and follow the same method as for chicken stock. Reduce the stock down to 6 ounces. Keep the stock clear, otherwise it will have to be clarified.

Compote of Rhubarb

    3 ounces raspberry vinegar
    3 ounces sugar
    1 pound washed, peeled and cubed rhubarb

Bring the vinegar and sugar to a boil. Add the rhubarb and simmer until just cooked. Remove from heat and refrigerate. Serve the compote very cold, with the terrine of duck.

Cream of Bay Scallops and Artichokes

    36 bay scallops
    salt and pepper
    $1^1/_2$ ounces unsalted butter
    $1^1/_2$ ounces shallots, finely chopped
    6 ounces artichoke hearts, diced
    6 ounces dry white wine
    3 cups fish stock (see below)
    3 cups Crème Fraîche
    1 ounce cognac

Season the scallops with salt and pepper. Set aside. In a saucepan, melt the butter and add shallots. Sauté until tender and translucent but not browned. Add the scallops, artichoke hearts and white wine. Cook over medium heat about 1 minute. Remove the scallops and artichoke hearts to a platter. Add the fish stock (recipe below) to the pan and reduce the liquid to about 4 ounces, skimming off impurities frequently while reducing. When reduced, add the Crème Fraîche. Bring to a boil and simmer for one minute.

Strain the liquid through a fine sieve or a piece of cheesecloth. In a second saucepan, reheat the scallops and artichoke hearts in cognac. Add the white wine/cream sauce and bring to a boil. Simmer for one minute. Correct seasoning and serve immediately.

Fish Stock

> 4 ounces unsalted butter
> 3 pounds fish bones and trimmings, preferably from sole
> or other white flat fish
> $1/2$ pound sliced onions
> 4 ounces white leeks
> 2 ounces parsley stalks
> 1 bay leaf
> $1/2$ bottle white wine
> 4 quarts cold water

Melt the butter in a stockpot. Add the fish bones, onions, leeks, parsley, bay leaf and peppercorns. Let simmer for 5 minutes, stirring frequently. Moisten with white wine. Simmer for another 5 minutes. Add the cold water. Bring to a boil, skim off impurities and then simmer 20 minutes. Pass through a fine sieve or cheesecloth. Makes approximately 4 quarts.

Rack of Lamb Elizabeth

> three 8–10 ounce eyes of lamb from a rack of lamb
> rosemary and thyme
> 6 ounces olive oil
> salt and pepper
> three 4 ounce rectangles of puff pastry (see below)
> 6 ounces spinach purée (see below)
> 6 ounces duxelles (see below)
> egg wash
> 12 ounces Madeira sauce (see below)

Trim the eyes of lamb. Sprinkle with rosemary and thyme. Marinate the lamb in olive oil for 12 hours, turning every 3 hours. Then season with salt and pepper. Sear the lamb quickly on all sides at high heat in a skillet, making sure not to cook the lamb. Cool.

Roll the puff pastry into 3 rectangles. The length of each rectangle should be approximately 3 inches longer than the length of each eye of lamb and the width of each rectangle should be approximately 4 times the width of each of the eyes of lamb. Place the spinach purée in the center of the rectangle, spreading the length of the lamb. Spread the duxelles on top of the spinach purée. Place the lamb in the center of each rectange on top of the duxelles. Egg wash the edges of the puff pastry. Fold the puff pastry to enclose the lamb and seal the edges. Place the pastries on a baking sheet and egg wash the top and sides. Allow to rest a minimum of 10 minutes before baking. Place in a preheated 400° oven and bake 20 minutes. The pastries will be golden brown and the lamb pink. Remove from the oven and let rest for 5 minutes. Cut each rectangle into 8 slices (4 per serving). Serve with Madeira sauce.

Puff Pastry

8 ounces flour
5 ounces ice-cold water
8 ounces unsalted butter
pinch of salt
few drops of lemon juice

Sift the flour and the salt. Blend in 2 ounces of unsalted butter. Add the lemon juice to the water. Make a well in the center of the flour and pour in the water and lemon juice. Knead well. Add more flour if necessary. Shape the dough into a ball and wrap in foil or wax paper. Allow the dough to rest in a cool place for approximately 30 minutes. Cut a cross halfway through the dough and pull out the corners to form a star. Roll out the points of the star, leaving the center thick. Knead the remaining 6 ounces of unsalted butter to the same texture as the dough. This is *most* important. Place the butter on the center square, which is 4 times thicker than the flaps. Fold over the flaps. Roll out to a rectangle approximately 12 inch by 6 inch; cover with a cloth and let rest for 5 to 10 minutes in a cool place. Then roll out approximately 24 inch by 8 inch, fold both ends to the center, fold in half again to form a square. This is one double turn. Allow to rest in a cool place for approximately 20 minutes. Turn the dough once to either the right or the left. Roll out to approximately 24 inch by 6 inch. Give one more double turn and allow to rest for another 20 minutes. Give two more double turns, allowing to rest between each process, following the same procedure. Then allow to rest before using. Care must be taken when rolling out the dough to keep the ends and sides square. Yields 16 ounces of puff pastry.

Note: This can be prepared in the morning and then baked just prior to serving.

Spinach Purée

> 15 ounces fresh spinach
> salt and pepper
> pinch of nutmeg

Remove all stalks from the spinach leaves and wash thoroughly. Cook the spinach quickly in boiling, salted water until tender. Refresh under cold water. Drain and squeeze all liquid from the spinach. Purée the spinach in a food processor or blender. Season with salt, pepper and pinch of nutmeg. Yields about 6 ounces.

Duxelles

> $1^1/_2$ ounces unsalted butter
> $1^1/_2$ ounces finely chopped shallots
> 12 ounces finely chopped mushroom caps and stalks
> 3 ounces dry white wine
> salt and pepper

Heat the butter in a saucepan. Add the shallots and mushrooms, making sure not to brown the shallots. Add the white wine. Cook vigorously, stirring constantly, until all the liquid is evaporated and the mixture is dry. Correct the seasoning. Yields approximately 6 ounces of duxelles.

Madeira Sauce

> 3 ounces unsalted butter
> $1^1/_2$ ounces chopped shallots
> 6 ounces dry Madeira
> $4^1/_2$ cups brown fond de veau (see below)
> $1^1/_2$ ounces Crème Fraîche
> salt and pepper

Melt $1^1/_2$ ounces of unsalted butter in a saucepan. Add the shallots and sauté until tender and translucent but not browned. Add the Madeira. Reduce the Madeira until it is nearly evaporated. Add the fond de veau (recipe follows) and reduce it to approximately 6 ounces, skimming off impurities frequently while reducing. When reduced, add the Crème Fraîche. Simmer for 1 minute. Beat the $1^1/_2$ ounces of remaining butter by bits into the sauce and correct the seasoning. When the butter is incorporated and the sauce is of the consistency to coat the back of a spoon, strain in a fine sieve. Yields approximately $1^1/_2$ cups.

Fond de Veau (Brown)

$7^1/_2$ pounds veal bones	$3/_4$ pound overripe tomatoes
6 ounces celery stalks	$4^1/_2$ ounces tomato paste
12 ounces onions	36 peppercorns
12 ounces carrots	3 bay leaves
9 ounces white leeks	6 quarts cold water
$1^1/_2$ garlic cloves	

Brown the veal bones in the oven. Sauté the celery stalks, onions, carrots, white leeks and garlic in oil. Add the vegetables to the veal bones in a stockpot. Add the tomatoes and the tomato paste, thyme, peppercorns and bay leaves. Cover with water. Bring to a boil and then simmer for 5 hours, skimming off impurities frequently. Pass through a sieve or cheesecloth. Produces about 6 cups.

Watercress Purée

3 large bunches of watercress, washed
1 ounce parsley, cleaned
2 ounces finely chopped Bermuda onions
1 ounce butter
3 ounces Crème Fraîche
salt, pepper, nutmeg
1 tablespoon lemon juice
roasted pine nuts

Cut off the bunch of watercress just above the point where the stems join the leaves. Blanche watercress and parsley. Sauté Bermuda onions in butter, cooking until onion is transparent but not browned. Add watercress, parsley and 1 ounce of Crème Fraîche and bring to a boil. Season with salt, pepper and nutmeg.

Place all ingredients in a blender or food processor and purée. Finish off with lemon juice and Crème Fraîche. Correct seasoning and consistency. Serve immediately. Dish cannot be held in bain marie as it will discolor. Garnish with toasted pine nuts.

CELERIAC PURÉE

1 pound diced celeriac (celery roots)
4 ounces potatoes, peeled and chopped
3 cups milk
salt and pepper
3 large cooking apples, peeled and chopped
3 ounces Crème Fraîche

Place celeriac, potatoes and milk in a saucepan. Season with salt and pepper. Cook for approximately 15 minutes. Add diced apples and continue to cook 5 minutes more. Strain off cooking liquid and reserve. Place celeriac, potatoes and apples in blender or food processor. Add Crème Fraîche and purée. Correct seasoning and consistency (i.e., if too thick, add some of cooking liquid). Serve immediately. Purée may also be kept warm in bain marie. Garnish with finely diced raw apple.

LEMON JAPONAIS WITH STRAWBERRY PURÉE

5 egg whites
8 ounces sugar
1 ounce flour
3 ounces finely grated almonds
4 ounces finely grated hazelnuts
pinch of cornstarch

Beat the egg whites until stiff. Add 2 ounces of the sugar and continue beating until the sugar is thoroughly blended. Combine separately the flour, hazelnuts, almonds, cornstarch and remaining sugar. Fold this mixture into the egg whites.

Place the mixture in a pastry bag fitted with a flat nozzle. Pipe the mixture into approximately 4 inch diameter rounds on a buttered baking sheet.

Bake in a preheated 350° oven for 15 to 20 minutes until golden brown and crisp. Let cool. When cool, spread each round with lemon cream (recipe below). It should have a mirror finish.

Serve japonais on individual dessert plates. Cover the plate with the coulis des fraises (puréed strawberries) (recipe below) and place the lemon japonais in the center.

Lemon Cream

> juice of 2 lemons
> $2^1/_2$ ounces sugar
> 2 eggs
> $2^1/_2$ ounces unsalted butter

Place all ingredients in a saucepan and slowly bring to a simmer, stirring constantly. Simmer for one minute. Remove from heat and let cool.

Puréed Strawberries

> 20 medium-sized strawberries
> 1 ounce eau de vie de framboise (liqueur)
> 4 ounces Crème Fraîche

Purée all ingredients together in a blender or food processor.

CANTINA D'ITALIA

1214-A 18th Street, N.W. · Washington, D.C. · (202) 659-1830

In 1968, Washingtonians had their first exposure to fine Italian cuisine. Cantina d'Italia opened. It soon gained recognition as a four-star restaurant, demonstrating that membership in this elite category is not limited to French restaurants.

Frequent diners at Cantina will always find something new and different to experience. The menu is constantly changing, yet the high standard of excellence prevails.

Cantina's menu is Northern Italian. The dinner that follows is a typical dinner that would be served in the Piemonte region of Italy. It begins with an antipasto followed by a veal dish, "Scaloppe di Vitello Come Piace a Kilpatrick." Owner Joseph de Asserta specifically chose this to be included in the book in honor of columnist James J. Kilpatrick, one of his favorite customers.

Instead of the usual pasta accompaniment, rice was selected in keeping with the Piemontese tradition. Rice grows in abundance in this area. It is cooked in Barolo wine, giving it a rich and full flavor.

What better way to complete this Italian dinner than with Zabaione? Prepare at the table for added elegance.

Cantina d'Italia

Gattinara

Pepperoni
(Cold antipasto)

Risotto al Barolo
(Barolo Rice)

Scaloppe di Vitello Come Piace a
"Kilpatrick"
(Veal Scallopine)

Zabaione

Cold Antipasto

A proper introduction to a traditional Italian meal is a simple antipasto.

$^1/_2$ cup Italian olive oil
3 large fresh red peppers
12 anchovy fillets

In a frying pan, heat oil until very hot. Add sliced and seeded peppers, skin side down. Cook for 5 to 7 minutes; stir, coating with the oil. Remove from heat and drain on paper towels. When cool, place in refrigerator and chill.

To serve, arrange peppers and anchovies in a crisscross design on a platter. Enjoy a truly great combination of taste as is, or dress with oil and vinegar.

Barolo Rice

$^1/_2$ stick of butter
1 medium yellow onion, finely chopped
$1^1/_2$ cups arborio rice
1 cup seasoned chicken broth
1 bottle Barolo wine
1 cup grated fresh parmesan cheese

In a large frying pan, add the finely chopped onion and 3 tablespoons of butter. Sauté over medium heat until golden. Add rice and broth, stirring constantly with a wooden spoon so rice does not burn. When all of the broth has been absorbed, add 3 cups of wine. Continue to stir until rice is tender, 20 to 25 minutes.

When ready to serve, stir in 1 tablespoon of butter and 1 cup of parmesan cheese.

Note: As rice cooks it may require additional wine. Rice when cooked should be moist, not dry.

Veal Scallopine

$^1/_4$ pound unsalted butter
1 teaspoon Italian olive oil
1 cup scallions, finely chopped
1 cup heavy cream
3 teaspoons Dijon mustard
veal for 6, pounded and dredged in flour on one side
salt and pepper to taste

To prepare this dish you will use 2 large iron skillets. Keep 1 over high heat until ready to serve. Place the second skillet over medium heat and sauté scallions in butter along with the olive oil. The oil will prevent the butter from burning. Allow to cook for 7 to 10 minutes, then add the heavy cream and mustard. Whisk until well blended. Raise the heat to high and add the veal. Cook approximately 6 to 8 minutes, turning the veal over in sauce at least once. Season with salt and pepper. Transfer to the first pan and serve at once.

Zabaione

6 egg yolks
1 whole egg
6 tablespoons of sugar
6 ounces of golden Creme Florio Marsala wine

Beat egg yolks and whole egg in a metal bowl over low heat. Gradually add, while beating, the sugar and the wine. Continue beating vigorously wth a wire whisk until mixture begins to thicken. Do not overcook. Texture should be light and foamy. Serve warm in wine or sherbet glasses.

Chez Andrée

10 East Glebe Road · Alexandria, Virginia · (703) 836-1404

Excellent cuisine can be found in places other than George-town, Old Town and "restaurant row." Chez Andrée, in an unpretentious location in Alexandria, is worth looking for. It is not far from Old Town in an unassuming building on Glebe Road. The warm country style interior, the personalized and friendly service and fine French food more than make up for the exterior.

You will be greeted by at least one member of the Lecureux family, all of whom take pride and part in their restaurant. The atmosphere is low-keyed and marked by happy, friendly people committed to making your evening a pleasant one.

The recipe for the country pâté that follows is one that took over a year to secure. Madame Lecureux had first tasted it in a market in France. The merchant would not release the recipe. Her mother inquired in the town and was able to locate the woman who made the pâté, who, after much coaxing, finally turned over the recipe. If you have shied away from making pâté in the past, you will find this recipe surprisingly simple. After tasting, you will understand why Madame Lecureux had to have it.

We felt the same way about Chez Andrée's house dressing. After much soul-searching, Madame Lecureux finally turned over her recipe to us for this cookbook!

Chez Andrée

White Graves	Pâté Breton
Pomerol Château	Bordeaux Civet de Lapin (Rabbit in Red Wine Sauce)
Trotonoy	Vinaigrette Sauce with Avocado
	Crème Caramel

Pâté Breton

250 grams pork liver (approximately $^1/_2$ pound)
250 grams fresh fat back
500 grams pork butt
3 cloves garlic
3 shallots
1 teaspoon pepper
bouquet garni

Preheat oven to 350°.

Grind all of the above ingredients together in a food processor or meat grinder. If using a meat grinder, it is suggested that you put the mixture through twice.

To cook, place the mixture in a terrine or glass bread pan. Top with bouquet garni and cover with foil. Set the terrine in a shallow pan of water. The water should come about halfway up the outside of the terrine. Bake in lower third of the oven for approximately $1^1/_2$ hours. Remove foil for part of the baking time to brown the top. When done, remove terrine from the water bath and allow to cool for several hours at room temperature, then chill.

Rabbit in Red Wine Sauce

one 3-pound rabbit, cleaned, dressed and disjointed
$1/4$ cup bacon, cut up
$1/2$ cup butter
1 medium onion, chopped
3 tablespoons flour
$1^{1}/_{2}$ cup dry red wine
2 cups chicken broth or water
$1/2$ teaspoon salt and $1/8$ teaspoon pepper
bouquet garni (bay leaves, thyme, parsley)
1 pound mushrooms, quartered

Clean the rabbit pieces with a damp towel and allow to dry. In a skillet over medium heat, brown rabbit pieces with bacon in butter. Remove rabbit and bacon pieces and set aside. Add onions to pan and brown in drippings. Add flour and stir well. When blended, gradually pour in wine and chicken broth, stirring constantly. Season with salt and pepper.

Return rabbit pieces and bacon to the pan and add bouquet garni. Cover and cook for 1 hour over low heat. Five minutes before serving add the mushrooms.

Vinaigrette Sauce with Avocado

1 egg
1 rounded tablespoon Dijon mustard
$1^{1}/_{2}$ cup vegetable oil
$1/4$ cup white vinegar
$1/2$ teaspoon salt and $1/2$ teaspoon white pepper
3 avocados

In a bowl, blend egg and mustard together. Slowly add oil and vinegar. Season with salt and pepper. Pour over halved avocados.

If you wish to substitute a green salad for the avocado salad, we highly recommend the house dressing.

House Dressing

1 pint mayonnaise
1 cup vegetable oil
2 rounded tablespoons Dijon mustard
1 rounded teaspoon minced garlic
3 tablespoons white vinegar
1 rounded teaspoon salt
$^1/_4$ teaspoon ground black pepper

Place mayonnaise in mixer and slowly blend in oil. Add Dijon mustard and garlic. Gradually add vinegar, blending well. Season with salt and pepper.

Crème Caramel

$1^1/_2$ cups sugar
1 quart milk
4 eggs
1 teaspoon vanilla
6 custard cups

Preheat oven to 325°. Melt 1 cup sugar in a heavy-bottomed skillet, without stirring, over medium heat. When the sugar turns a caramel color, pour into custard cups and swirl around to coat the bottom and sides. Place cups in shallow baking dish and set aside.

Pour milk in a saucepan and place over low heat. Slowly stir in $^1/_2$ cup sugar. Stir well then set aside to cool.

Beat eggs in a large bowl and slowly add the cooled milk-sugar mixture. Continue beating until smooth. Stir in the vanilla. Pour the custard into the caramel lined cups and bake in a water bath at 325° for 1 hour. Cool and unmold on dessert plates.

EL TIO PEPE

2809 M Street, N.W. · Washington, D.C. · (202) 337-0730

In a city where ethnic restaurants abound, diners do not have to go abroad to enjoy a good pasta, Peking duck or paella. The latter can be found at El Tio Pepe's, a two-story Spanish restaurant in Georgetown. It serves the best paella in town and entertains you with flamenco dancing and guitar.

There are many versions of paella. The ingredients vary depending on the meat, fowl, fish and vegetables that happen to be available. El Tio Pepe's recipe is best prepared in a paella pan but can be made in an iron skillet. It is an unusual dish.

For a truly Spanish evening, begin with Gazpacho, a cold vegetable soup that is essentially a liquid salad, and close with a rich Catalonian style custard.

EL TIO PEPE

Torres Gran Viña Sol

Gazpacho a la Andaluza

Paella a la Valenciana

Crema a la Catalana
(Soft Custard, Catalonian Style)

Gazpacho a la Andaluza

3 tablespoons red wine vinegar
4 cups cold water
2 cups Italian bread cubes, crusts removed
1 medium cucumber, peeled, seeded and diced
8 tomatoes, peeled and seeded
1 medium-sized onion, chopped
1 large green pepper, seeded
2 teaspoons chopped garlic
1 teaspoon cumin
4 tablespoons olive oil
1 tablespoon Spanish paprika
salt

Garnish

$^1\!/_2$ cup bread cubes
1 small cucumber, diced
1 small onion, chopped
1 green pepper, chopped
2 tablespoons olive oil

In a large bowl combine red wine vinegar and cold water. Add the bread cubes and allow to soak for a few minutes. Add the remaining ingredients and mix well. Purée in a blender and strain the mixture through a fine sieve. Season with salt to taste. Chill in the refrigerator until ready to serve.

Brown the $^1\!/_2$ cup bread cubes in oil. Serve gazpacho chilled, garnishing each portion with the bread cubes, cucumber, onions and green pepper.

Paella a la Valenciana

1$\frac{1}{2}$ pound chicken
4 tablespoons olive oil
1 pound lean pork, cubed
1 medium onion, chopped
1 green pepper, seeded and chopped
5 cloves garlic, finely chopped
3 tomatoes, peeled and chopped
$\frac{1}{2}$ pound chorizo (Spanish sausage), sliced
1 pound squid, cleaned and sliced
2 cups long grain rice
1 tablespoon Spanish paprika
4 cups chicken stock
$\frac{1}{4}$ teaspoon saffron threads
18 medium-sized raw shrimp, peeled and deveined
6 clams in the shell, scrubbed and steamed 5 minutes
12 mussels in the shell, scrubbed and steamed 5 minutes
$\frac{1}{2}$ cup green peas
$\frac{1}{2}$ cup pimentos
salt

Garnish

parsley
lemon wedges

Paella is best prepared in a paellero, the vessel that gives this dish its name. A casserole 16 inches in diameter and 2$\frac{1}{2}$ inches deep may be substituted.

Cut the chicken into medium-sized serving pieces. Heat the oil in the skillet and add chicken, frying until brown. Remove the chicken. Add the pork and, again, fry until brown. Remove pork and add the onions, green pepper and garlic. Sauté until they are soft. Add the tomatoes and fry for an additional two minutes. This mixture is referred to as the "sofrito."

Return the chicken and pork to the pan and add the sliced chorizo and squid and cook for 10 minutes. Add the rice and paprika and mix well. Cook for 5 minutes.

Add chicken stock and saffron. On top of rice lay shrimp, clams, mussels, pimentos and green peas. Season with salt to taste.

Cook for 20 minutes. For the last 10 minutes place in a 350° oven. When ready to serve, garnish with lemon wedges and parsley.

CUSTARD, CATALONIAN STYLE

4 cups milk
1 vanilla bean
1 lemon
14 egg yolks
1½ cups sugar
2 tablespoons cornstarch

In a saucepan, scald the milk. Add the vanilla bean and the peel of half a lemon. Remove from heat.

In a mixing bowl, beat the egg yolks, cornstarch and sugar (reserving 3 tablespoons of sugar) until slightly thick. Transfer mixture to a heavy-bottomed saucepan and, over low heat, slowly pour in the hot milk, stirring constantly. Continue cooking over low heat until the custard coats a spoon. Do not let the mixture boil or the eggs will curdle. Spoon the custard into dessert dishes and sprinkle with sugar. Sear the top to a golden brown color. The chef suggests using a red hot piece of iron to burn the surface. We have found placing the custard under the broiler in an oven to be equally successful.

Chill custard and serve with lady fingers.

GERMAINE'S

2400 Wisconsin Avenue, N.W. · Washington, D.C. · (202) 965-1185

A relative newcomer to the Washington restaurant scene is Germaine's. Already it has established itself as one of *the* places to dine. The reason—superb Asian cuisine.

The restaurant developed from Germaine Swanson's dissatisfaction with the Oriental food being served in local restaurants. Although Germaine's father owned a restaurant in Vietnam, she did not learn to cook there. When she came to Washington in 1971, what she knew about cooking she remembered from her grandmother. Her reputation as a Vietnamese cook grew and soon she was teaching classes in her home. Opening a restaurant was inevitable.

The menu boasts forty entrées, mostly Vietnamese, with Korean and Thai accents.

The well-spaced tables in the two dining rooms provide a special attraction. Here one can carry on a private conversation in a relaxed yet elegant atmosphere.

The Vietnamese spring rolls suggested as an appetizer would also be an excellent hors d'oeuvre at a party.

The Basil Beef can be made by substituting chicken, which is equally good.

GERMAINE'S

Château la Noe Muscadet 1979	Spring Rolls
Burgess Cellar Petite Siran 1976 or Trentadue Winery Zinfandel 1974	Basil Beef or Chicken
Joseph Phelps Gewürztraminer 1979	Pumpkin Custard

SPRING ROLLS

(makes 60–70 pieces)
1 pound medium-sized raw shrimp, chopped, or 1 pound fresh crab meat
$\frac{1}{2}$ cup wood ears or dried mushrooms
4 ounces clear (mung bean) noodles
1 pound fresh bean sprouts or finely shredded carrot
1 pound lean ground pork
1 large onion, chopped
1 bundle green onion (scallion), chopped
1 whole egg
$\frac{1}{2}$ teaspoon black or white pepper
$\frac{1}{2}$ teaspoon salt
30–35 sheets rice paper, cut into halves
a bowl of warm water
5 cups vegetable cooking oil

Clean and devein the shrimp. Chop into small pieces. Soak wood ears or mushrooms in warm water for 15 minutes. Clean, chop and drain well.

Soak clear noodles also in warm water for 15 minutes. Cut into lengths 1 inch long and drain well.

Wash bean sprouts or carrot with cold water. Drain and cut into lengths 1 inch long.

Combine all the ingredients in a large bowl and set aside. Lay a half sheet of rice paper on a clean kitchen cloth. Moisten your fingers in a bowl of water and wet the rice paper thoroughly. Fold the rice paper in half and set aside for a few minutes to soften.

Set 1 tablespoon of mixed ingredients on the middle of the rice paper and roll diagonally into a cylinder. Set aside for deep frying.

Heat the vegetable oil to 325° in a regular frying pan. Fry a few rolls at a time until golden brown. Serve hot or at room temperature with purchased fish sauce.

Note: Spring rolls can be prepared in advance and frozen for future use. Simply defrost and reheat in 400° oven for 5 minutes.

BASIL CHICKEN OR BEEF

12 chicken breast halves or 3 pounds lean sirloin tip beef
9 tablespoons vegetable oil
3 teaspoons cornstarch mixed with water (optional)

SAUCE

$1^1/_2$ ounces dried oriental sweel basil leaves, soaked in water for $^1/_2$ hour and drained
$1^1/_2$ teaspoons finely chopped ginger
$1^1/_2$ teaspoons finely chopped garlic
3 oriental red peppers (fresh), seeded and chopped
3 tablespoons Thai chili sauce
3 tablespoons sugar
6 tablespoons light soy sauce
6 tablespoons fish sauce
6 tablespoons dry sherry
12 tablespoons water

Combine all the sauce ingredients and marinate at least 4 hours, or overnight to get the full flavor of the basil leaves.

Bone and skin chicken breasts. Finely shred the chicken into 2-inch strips. If substituting the beef, clean the fat and grissel from the beef before shredding into 2-inch long pieces.

Heat wok with cooking oil to 400°. Add chicken (beef) and give a quick stir fry. Turn the heat down to medium while stirring the chicken (beef) until done. Add sauce and cook for 2 additional minutes (add cornstarch to thicken sauce if desired).

Transfer the basil chicken or beef to a serving platter and serve hot with steamed rice.

PUMPKIN CUSTARD

1 young pumpkin (around 5–6 pounds) or individual acorn squashes
4 eggs
1 cup water
1 cup fresh coconut cream
$1/2$ can condensed milk

Cut off the top of the pumpkin or acorn squashes and scoop out the seeds and pulp, reserving the top for later use. Beat the eggs lightly; add water, coconut cream and milk. Strain the mixture through a sieve or food mill and add to the pumpkin or squash shells.

Set up a steamer. Place the shells in a large bowl and steam for $1^{1}/_{2}$ hours. Chill, slice and serve cold.
Note: Do not eat the skins.

HARVEY'S

1001 Eighteenth Street, N.W. · Washington, D.C. · (202) 833-1858

The year 1858 is an important year in Washington D.C.'s history. Construction was beginning on the Washington monument and T.M. Harvey's Ladies and Gentleman's Oyster Saloon opened. Nine years later the saloon moved to larger quarters and became known as Harvey's. Lincoln set the tradition for Presidents dining at Harvey's. It is known today as "the restaurant of the Presidents."

Harvey's provides more than an interesting parade of famous faces. It happens to be the best seafood restaurant in town.

Alex Stuart, the present owner, has planned a seafood dinner beginning with his famous Crab Gumbo. The main entrée, Crabmeat with Smithfield Ham, is served with a cold cucumber salad and zucchini with walnuts and herbs. Dinner guests have often requested these recipes. Most guests understood and accepted our commitment to withhold them until the publication of this book. The desire for the zucchini recipe, however, drove one of our guests to the kitchen, where she was caught going through the spice cabinet. She will be delighted to see this book in print!

HARVEY'S

Chardonnay, Robert
Mondavi

Crab Gumbo

Cucumber Salad

Fresh Crabmeat and Smithfield
Ham

Sautéed Fresh Zucchini with Walnuts

Mousse au Chocolat

CRAB GUMBO

2 teaspoons vegetable oil
1 small chopped onion
1 small green pepper, chopped
$1/4$ clove garlic, crushed and chopped
1 rib celery, diced
1 cup okra, chopped
10 ounce can tomatoes
$1/2$ teaspoon thyme
$1/4$ teaspoon basil
$1/4$ teaspoon fennel
1 bay leaf
1 tablespoon tomato purée
salt and tabasco to taste
$1/2$ teaspoon Worcestershire
$1/2$ cup clam juice
3 cups water
1 cup cooked rice
1 cup lump crabmeat, cleaned and slightly flaked

Heat oil in large pan. Add onion and green pepper and sauté
for 5 minutes over low heat. Add remaining ingredients except the

rice and crabmeat and simmer approximately 45 minutes. Remove the bay leaf and add rice and crabmeat. Simmer 10 minutes more.

CUCUMBER SALAD

4-5 cucumbers, peeled and thinly sliced
2 medium onions, thinly sliced
$1/4$ clove garlic
salt and pepper
Tabasco to taste
$1/3$ cup sugar
1 cup white vinegar
paprika and 6 tablespoons sour cream for garnish

Combine all ingredients in a glass bowl and mix thoroughly. Marinate in refrigerator at least 2 hours. Discard garlic. When ready to serve, arrange on individual plates and garnish with 1 tablespoon of sour cream. Sprinkle with paprika.
Note: Salad is best when allowed to marinate 1 or 2 days.

FRESH CRABMEAT AND SMITHFIELD HAM

8 10 tablespoons butter
2 pounds lump crab meat
1 teaspoon flour
6 ounces Smithfield ham, diced
$1/2$ teaspoon paprika
6 lemon wedges

Melt butter in large skillet. Add crabmeat, flour and ham. Sprinkle with paprika. Sauté until golden, adding more butter if necessary. Serve with lemon wedges.

Sautéed Fresh Zucchini with Walnuts

4–6 tablespoons butter
Herbes de Provence (if not available use thyme, basil,
savory, lavender and fennel)
salt and pepper
3 tablespoons walnuts, chopped and partially crushed
2 pounds fresh zucchini

Melt butter in skillet and add herbs, salt, pepper and walnuts. Finely slice unpeeled zucchini and add to pan. Cook over medium heat until al dente.

Mousse au Chocolat

4 squares unsweetened chocolate
4 egg yolks
$\frac{1}{2}$ teaspoon vanilla
1 pint heavy cream
6 ounces sugar
2 ounces coffee brandy (optional)
whipped cream and strawberries for garnish

Melt chocolate in a double boiler. In a mixing bowl beat yolks and vanilla for 3 to 4 minutes until light in color.

In a chilled bowl whip heavy cream until stiff peaks form. Fold into yolk mixture. Add the sugar and mix until blended. Remove bowl from mixer and quickly add the hot melted chocolate. Avoid pouring chocolate in one spot; use a circular motion to distribute chocolate evenly. It is important that melted chocolate be hot before adding to mixture. Pour in coffee brandy and stir until mixture reaches uniform chocolate color.

Chill in refrigerator for at least 1 hour before serving. Serve with whipped cream, and garnish with a strawberry on top.

THE INN AT LITTLE WASHINGTON

Washington, Virginia · (703) 675-3800

A change from the Washington dining scene is the Inn at Little Washington, Virginia. It should always be included with Washington's finest restaurants but remembered that it is in Washington, Virginia, seventy miles to the west.

All the touches one would find in a country inn are present—fresh flowers, homemade breads, herb butter, pastries and generous hospitality. The Inn has one thing more, superb cuisine. The menu has a definite French flavor but reflects a fresh imaginative approach to cooking. Many of the ingredients come from the farms, rivers and orchards of Rappahannock County.

The Inn's success is the result of the talents of the two proprietors, Patrick O'Connell and Reinhart Lynch, who also double as chef and maitre d'hotel. Patrick's imagination and expertise in the kitchen are complimented by Reinhart's savoir-faire in the dining room.

The menu changes with the season. When watercress is in season, don't miss the watercress soup. You may be surprised at the simplicity of this recipe.

Patrick, with his usual attention to detail, not only gave us his recipe for the Veal Shenandoah, but invited us into the kitchen for a demonstration. It will undoubtedly become one of your favorites—it is ours.

THE INN AT LITTLE WASHINGTON

Callaway Chenin Blanc
1976

Cream of Watercress Soup

Salad of Kiwi Fruit

Escalope de Veau Shenandoah

Fresh Pineapple Sherbet

CREAM OF WATERCRESS SOUP

9 tablespoons unsalted butter
$1^1/_2$ cups chopped onions
6 cups chopped, firmly packed, fresh watercress leaves
9 tablespoons flour
$8^1/_4$ cups boiling, rich chicken stock
$^3/_4$ teaspoon salt
freshly ground black pepper
$1^1/_2$ tablespoons sugar
egg yolk, beaten (optional)
$^3/_4$ cup heavy cream, whipped

In butter, sauté onions over low heat until they are translucent. Add watercress and stir until wilted. Blend in flour and cook gently for 5 minutes, stirring constantly. Pour in boiling stock and season with salt, pepper and sugar. Cook at a bare simmer for 45 minutes, stirring occasionally. Strain the soup through a sieve.

If soup is too thick, thin with a little cream. If you like a thicker soup, blend a little soup into a beaten egg yolk; stir back into soup and heat. Do not boil after adding the egg yolk. Whip the $^1/_2$ cup cream until it stands in soft peaks and fold into the hot soup just before serving. Garnish with fresh watercress leaves.

Salad of Kiwi Fruit

3 Belgium endives
3 kiwis
1 cup heavy cream
2 tablespoons lime juice
1 tablespoon lemon juice
1 tablespoon simple vinaigrette dressing
salt and white pepper to taste
nutmeg
$^1/_2$ cup pecan or walnut halves

Peel and thinly slice the kiwi. Arrange in flower design interspersed with spears of Belgium endive.

In small metal bowl, stir cream with whisk while slowly adding acids (lime, lemon and vinaigrette) in droplets until cream thickens naturally. Season with salt and pepper. Pour dressing over kiwi and endive. Garnish with nutmeg and either pecan or walnut halves.

Escalope de Veau Shenandoah

1 gallon fresh apple cider
1 teaspoon chopped shallots
6 cloves
$^1/_4$ cup brown sauce
$^1/_4$ cup heavy cream
Calvados apple brandy
8–10 tablespoons butter
flour for dredging
salt and pepper
veal cutlet for 6
3 Golden Delicious apples
sugar
cinnamon
nutmeg
lemon juice
finely chopped parsley

In large pan combine cider, shallots and cloves. Boil until liquid is reduced by half. Lower heat. Add brown sauce, which may be purchased at any gourmet market or made from beef or veal stock. Stir in heavy cream and splash with Calvados. Keep warm while preparing the veal.

Pound the veal lightly until very thin. Dredge with flour seasoned with salt and pepper. Heat 4 tablespoons butter in a hot skillet and when foam subsides add veal. Cook veal until lightly browned. Put aside on a warm platter and prepare apples.

Peel, core and halve apples. Slice approximately $1/4$ inch in thickness. In a large skillet, heat 4 tablespoons of butter. Add sliced apples and sprinkle with sugar, cinnamon and nutmeg. Drizzle apples with lemon juice to prevent browning. Toss frequently when apples begin to soften. Flambé with Calvados.

To serve, overlap sliced apples on veal in half moon design. Cover with sauce and garnish with chopped parsley.

Fresh Pineapple Sherbet

2 whole, fresh, ripe pineapples, peeled and puréed
$2/3$ cup of sugar for each cup of fruit purée
1 tablespoon of fresh lemon juice for each cup of fruit purée

Peel and core the pineapple and purée in a blender or food processor. Measure the purée, and for each cup add $2/3$ cup of sugar and 1 tablespoon of fresh lemon juice. Whip for several minutes to dissolve the sugar. Freeze in a stainless steel or ceramic bowl until almost set. Remove from the freezer and beat again until fluffy. Package in freezer containers and freeze. To serve, let the sherbet stand in the refrigerator for 15 minutes before serving.
Note: Chef O'Connell notes that any full-flavored, fresh and very ripe fruit purée can be used.

JACQUELINE'S

1990 M Street, N.W. · Washington, D.C. · (202) 785-8877

Jacqueline's, a very French restaurant, is owned and managed by Madame Jacqueline Rodier, a very French woman. She has been successful in a male dominated field because she involves herself in every aspect of the restaurant's operation.

The restaurant reflects her excellent taste. The bar has street signs from Paris and umbrellas from Paris cafés. One of the first benches used in the Paris subway is also a part of the alley setting.

The dining room, with brass chandeliers, stained glass windows and numerous antiques, creates an atmosphere of grace, warmth and gaiety. Diners can relax and enjoy an authentic French meal, which is exactly what Jacqueline's offers.

Her selection for this book includes Steak Jacqueline. It can be flambéed at the table, although her own spectacular showmanship is not necessary for this dish. It is an entrée that one would expect to be served in the finest Parisian restaurants. In a word, superb!

Jacqueline's

Châteauneuf-du-Pape   Fricassée d'Escargots au Cognac

Le Steak "Jacqueline"

Salade "Jacqueline"

Coupe "Jacqueline"

Fricassée d'Escargots au Cognac

3 tablespoons butter	4 large mushrooms, sliced
3 shallots, finely minced	salt and pepper to taste
36 snails, canned	1 cup heavy cream
2 tablespoons cognac	6 patty shells

Sauté finely chopped shallots in butter until tender but not brown. Add the snails, cognac, sliced mushrooms, salt and pepper. Blend in heavy cream and simmer. Stir frequently over very low heat. Be careful not to boil the mixture, since the cream will curdle. Taste for seasoning and serve in hot pastry shells that have been baked at 425° for 20 minutes.
Note: Patty shells may be purchased at a gourmet market or made from a basic puff pastry recipe.

Le Steak "Jacqueline"

1 cup brown sauce	1 tablespoon oil
6 tablespoons butter	12 Filet Mignon (4 ounces each)
1 pound mushrooms	$\frac{1}{2}$ cup brandy
2 teaspoons shallots	1 teaspoon Dijon mustard
1 teaspoon fresh garlic	$\frac{1}{2}$ cup heavy cream

Good quality brown stock is important, if not essential in French cooking. The classic brown sauce is the end product of a long simmered brown meat stock combined with various vegetables and herbs. A brown sauce may be purchased at a gourmet market or you may wish to make your own if time permits. Any French cookbook will include a recipe. Jacqueline's brown sauce, exquisite in taste, is the result of long hours in the kitchen. When time does not permit such luxury, Jacqueline suggests the following Easy Brown Sauce for home use.

EASY BROWN SAUCE

6 tablespoons flour
6 tablespoons butter
1 can Campbell's beef consommé

Blend butter and flour in saucepan over low heat and make a roux. Add hot consommé to the roux and bring to a boil. Lower heat and reduce liquid by one fourth. Set aside over low heat.

Sauté mushrooms, shallots and garlic in 4 tablespoons of butter. Add this mixture to your brown sauce.

In a large skillet place 2 tablespoons of butter and 1 tablespoon of oil over moderately high heat. When foam subsides add the fillets and sauté them on each side until done as desired. Season quickly with salt and pepper. Remove from heat and add brandy and flambé. When flame subsides, set steaks aside.

To your brown sauce, add heavy cream and mustard. Stir until well blended. Pour immediately over steaks and serve. Wild rice is a good accompaniment to this dish.

SALADE "JACQUELINE"

6 hearts of palm, quartered lengthwise
18 fresh mushrooms (sliced)
2 heads Boston lettuce
2 bunches watercress
12 ounces Jacqueline's French vinaigrette dressing

Arrange lettuce on individual salad plates. Distribute the hearts of palm and mushrooms over each plate. Pour the dressing over the salad and garnish with the watercress.

JACQUELINE'S FRENCH VINAIGRETTE DRESSING

1 egg yolk
1 whole egg
$^1/_2$ cup Dijon mustard
$1^1/_2$ cups red wine vinegar
$^3/_4$ teaspoon white pepper
$1^1/_2$ teaspoon salt
$^1/_2$ teaspoon finely minced shallots

$^1/_2$ teaspoon garlic
2 cups salad oil
$^1/_2$ cup olive oil

Combine in a bowl the eggs, mustard, vinegar, pepper, salt, shallots and garlic. Keep blending and slowly add the oils, pouring each in a very thin stream until mixture emulsifies. Place the dressing in a covered jar.

Keep refrigerated until ready to use. Extra dressing may be used on other salads. Shake well before serving.

COUPE "JACQUELINE"

3 pints vanilla ice cream
6 pears, diced
$1^1/_2$ ounces Ricard

$^1/_2$ ounce Grenadine
whipped cream
crushed ice

Chill dessert glasses. Fill large metal bowl with crushed ice. Place smaller metal bowl inside. Using a tablespoon, scoop ice cream into the smaller bowl. Dribble Ricard and Grenadine on ice cream and gently fold in the diced pears. Fill chilled glasses with ice cream mixture and immediately refrigerate in freezer for approximately 2 hours. A half hour before serving, transfer to the refrigerator. Top with fresh whipped cream.

JAPAN INN

1715 Wisconsin Avenue, N.W. · Washington, D.C. · (202) 337-3400

It is a fortunate aspect of the Washington community that it now has a first rate Japanese restaurant, the Japan Inn. Located in upper Georgetown, the restaurant is divided into three dining areas, each committed to a different style of Japanese food. In the Tempura Corner the chefs are continually preparing and serving their specialty, one piece at a time.

Steak, chicken or shrimp and Japanese vegetables are served in the Teppan-Yaki Room. On metal slabs in the center of each table, chefs with appropriate showmanship prepare bite-sized pieces, serving each guest as the foods are ready.

Sukiyaki and Shabu-Shabu are served in the traditional Japanese Room. This is a no-shoes area where diners are seated on mats on the floor.

For a Japanese meal at home, the Japan Inn recommends Tempura and Sukiyaki. The Tempura is light and delicate and is best prepared at the table. Sukiyaki should be served well cooked and flavored with soy sauce.

Japan Inn

Sake	Tempura
	Sukiyaki
	Ice Cream with Green Tea Liqueur

Tempura

12 large shrimp, shelled and deveined
3 green peppers, cut in 4 slices lengthwise
vegetable oil
$1/2$ cup flour

Batter (makes about 3 cups)

1 egg yolk	$1^2/_3$ cups flour
2 cups ice cold water	salt and pepper to taste
$1/_8$ teaspoon baking soda	12 lemon wedges

Dip shrimp in the flour and shake off any excess. Set aside. Combine egg yolk with water and baking soda in a large mixing bowl. Sift in the flour and mix well with a wooden spoon. The batter should be somewhat thin and watery and run easily off the spoon. The batter should not be made until ready to use.

Heat the oil until the temperature registers 375° on a deep-fat thermometer. Dip the shrimp and green peppers into the batter one piece at a time. Swirl the pieces around the batter to make sure they are well coated. Immediately drop into the hot oil. Turn the pieces with chopsticks or tongs after 1 minute and continue frying for an additional minute, or until light golden in color. To serve, sprinkle with salt and pepper and garnish with lemon wedges.

Note: Tempura must be served hot. The most practical way to do so is to prepare individual portions and serve immediately. Otherwise keep individual servings warm in the oven while remaining portions are being fried.

SUKIYAKI

2 pounds boneless lean beef (preferably tenderloin or sirloin)
$^3/_4$ cup water
One 10-ounce can shirataki (long noodlelike threads, drained)
1 can bamboo shoots
8 scallions, including 3 inches of the stem, cut into $1^1/_2$-inch pieces
1 medium-sized yellow onion, cut into $^1/_2$-inch thick slices
6 to 8 small white mushrooms, cut into $^1/_4$-inch thick slices
3 cakes tofu (soybean curd) cut into 1-inch cubes
3 ounces Chinese chrysanthemum leaves, watercress or Chinese cabbage
1 two-inch long strip beef fat, folded into a square
$^3/_4$ cup Japanese all-purpose soy sauce
6 to 9 tablespoons sugar
$^3/_4$ cup sake (rice wine)

Place the beef in a freezer for approximately 30 minutes, to make the slicing easier. Cut the beef against the grain, into slices $^1/_{10}$ of an inch thick.

Bring water to a boil and drop in the shirataki. Return to a second boil. Drain and cut the noodles into thirds. Scrape the bamboo shoots at the base. Cut in half lengthwise and slice into thin pieces. Run cold water over the slices and drain.

Arrange the meat, shirataki and vegetables attractively in separate rows on a large platter.

Preheat electric skillet to 425°. With chopsticks or tongs rub the folded strip of fat over the bottom of the hot skillet. Add 8 to 10 slices of beef. Pour in approximately $^1/_4$ cup of soy sauce and sprinkle the meat with 3 tablespoons of sugar. Cook for a minute, stir and turn the meat over. Push the meat to one side, adding about $^1/_3$ of the scallions, onions, mushrooms, tofu, shirataki, greens and bamboo shoots. Each vegetable should be cooked alongside the next, not mixed together. Pour in $^1/_4$ cup sake and $^1/_4$ cup of water. Cook for an additional 4 to 5 minutes.

Ice Cream with Green Tea Liqueur

6 scoops of vanilla ice cream
1 can mandarin oranges
green tea liqueur

Place the ice cream in individual dessert bowls. Form a circle with the mandarin oranges around the ice cream and pour green tea liqueur on top.

JEAN PIERRE

1835 K Street, N.W. · Washington, D.C. · (202) 466-2022

When one thinks of the fine French restaurants of Washington, Jean Pierre is bound to come to mind. It has been consistently chosen as a favorite restaurant by the dining-out regulars and for obvious reasons. Neither food nor service has failed over the years.

To prepare the palate for the lamb meal to follow, oysters with champagne are the perfect first course.

A fresh spinach salad with hazelnuts and a simple dressing enhance the flavor of lamb fillets that are seasoned to perfection.

A soufflé can be a delight at any dinner party. Attention is the most necessary ingredient. Soufflés are simple to prepare, yet your guests will respond as though you've whipped up something particularly special for them. And with this recipe you have!

Jean Pierre

Coteaux Champenois	Belons au Champagne
Château Beychevelle	Filet d'Agneau à l'Ail (Lamb Fillet with Garlic)
	Salade d'Epinards au Noix (Spinach Salad with Hazelnuts)
Champagne Brut	Bavarois à l'Orange (Orange Bavarian Cream)

Belons au Champagne

24 Belons oysters
$^1/_2$ liter champagne (brut)
2 shallots, puréed
1 cup fish Velouté (recipe below)
2 leeks, cut into julienne strips
white wine for cooking
3 tablespoons Hollandaise sauce
2 tablespoons whipped cream

Add the oysters, champagne and shallots to a saucepan over low heat. Cover and simmer for 20 minutes. Strain, reserving the liquid. Keep the oysters warm. Bring reserved liquid to a boil. Add the fish Velouté and bring to a second boil. Set aside. Cook the leeks with white wine in a covered saucepan until tender.

Place the leeks in the oyster shells. Top with the oysters. Cover with the reserved sauce, Hollandaise and whipped cream. Glaze in the oven just before serving.

Fish Velouté (1 cup)

1 tablespoon butter
$1^1/_2$ tablespoon flour
1 cup boiling fish stock

In a saucepan over low heat, melt the butter. Blend in the flour and cook slowly, stirring until the butter and flour are well blended (2 minutes). Remove from heat and pour in the boiling fish stock. Beat with a whisk. Boil for 1 minute, and continue stirring.

Lamb Fillet with Garlic

3 pounds fillet lamb
salt and pepper
nut oil
2 tablespoons butter
$1^1/_4$ cup white wine

3 heads garlic
1 carrot, sliced
1 onion, chopped
1 cup brown stock

Salt and pepper both sides of lamb. Cook in a frying pan with very hot nut oil. The lamb should be cooked until desired doneness. Drain the oil from the pan and set the lamb aside. Add butter to the pan and $^1/_4$ cup of white wine. Slowly cook the carrots, onion and 1 head of finely chopped garlic. Add the brown stock and the remaining 1 cup of white wine. Reduce the sauce and strain through a fine sieve. Serve lamb with the two heads of garlic (cooked in 350° oven in aluminum foil) and the sauce.

Spinach Salad with Hazelnuts

1 pound spinach
1 cup hazelnuts, finely chopped
1 teaspoon Dijon mustard
juice of 3 lemons
salt and pepper
$^1/_2$ cup ground nut oil

Wash and dry the spinach and discard the stems. Break into bite-sized pieces. Toss in a salad bowl with the hazelnuts.

Mix in a separate bowl mustard, lemon juice, salt and pepper. Slowly add the nut oil and blend well. Pour over the spinach and toss until all leaves are coated.

Orange Bavarian Cream

$^1/_2$ quart (2 cups) milk
$^1/_2$ teaspoon vanilla extract
$1^1/_2$ tablespoons ($^3/_4$ package) gelatin
9 egg yolks
$^1/_2$ pound (8 ounces) sugar
$^1/_2$ quart (2 cups) heavy cream
$^1/_4$ cup Cointreau
1 whole orange, cut in small pieces

In a saucepan bring milk and vanilla to a boil. Add gelatin and stir. Set aside. Beat egg yolks in a bowl. Gradually add the sugar to the yolks and continue beating for 2 to 3 minutes until the mixture is pale yellow. Pour into a saucepan over moderate heat. Gradually beat the milk mixture into the sugar-yolk mixture. Stir with a wooden spoon until mixture thickens enough to coat a spoon lightly. Let it cool. Beat the cream until it forms soft peaks. Add the Cointreau and orange pieces. Fold the whipped cream mixture into the cooled custard. Turn the Bavarian cream into a mold and chill in the refrigerator for approximately 4 hours.

THE JOCKEY CLUB

2100 Massachusetts Avenue, N.W. · Washington, D.C. · (202) 659-8000

Jockey Club, once the most popular place during the Kennedy administration, is located in the Fairfax Hotel on Embassy Row. Still the place for posh people, the Jockey Club has gone through some changes—new management and some refurbishing.

It remains one of the richest looking dining rooms in Washington, with its carved wood panels and dark beamed ceiling. The lighting is dim and the atmosphere intimate.

The menu is impressive, offering a choice of nearly twenty appetizers, ranging from Imperial Beluga Caviar to Mushrooms à la Daum. The Baked Crab Jockey is particularly good and was chosen as the appetizer for this book. The range of entrées makes selection difficult, but the waiters are very helpful. Trust their recommendations. For chocolate lovers the Chocolate Pot de Crème is a must.

The Jockey Club

Riesling Hugel 1975

Baked Crab Jockey

Spinach, Mushroom and Bacon Salad

Meursault Louis Latour 1977

Escalope de Veau Orloff (Veal Scallops Orloff)

Pot de Crème au Chocolat

Baked Crab Jockey

2 shallots, finely chopped
2 tablespoons butter
1 teaspoon curry powder
1 pound lump crab meat
salt and pepper
10 ounces white wine fish sauce (recipe below)
4 ounces whipped heavy cream
2 ounces Hollandaise sauce

Sauté the shallots in butter, adding curry, crabmeat, salt and pepper. Stir in the white wine sauce and bring to a boil. Remove from heat and fold in the whipped cream and Hollandaise sauce.

Spoon into Coquille St.-Jacques shells and glaze in oven just before serving.

White Wine Fish Sauce

1 cup fish fumet
1 pint heavy cream

3 tablespoons butter
4 tablespoons flour

In a saucepan, bring fish fumet (fish stock) to a boil. Reduce to $^1/_2$ cup. Add heavy cream and then add the roux (butter and flour blended together in a small frying pan over medium heat). Simmer for 20 minutes. Strain through a sieve.

FISH FUMET (STOCK)

    2 pounds fish bones
    1 onion
    $^1/_2$ lemon
    thyme, bay leaf, salt and pepper
    1 cup white wine

In a stockpot, place fish bones, onion, lemon, thyme, bay leaf, salt and pepper. Add the white wine and enough water to cover the bones. Boil for 20 minutes. Strain through a fine sieve.

SPINACH, MUSHROOM AND BACON SALAD

    2 pounds spinach
    1 pound mushrooms, sliced
    $^1/_2$ pound cooked bacon, chopped
    6 ounces house dressing (recipe below)

Wash the spinach well in 3 different water baths. Spin dry and place in salad bowl.

Heat the house dressing with the bacon; do not boil. Just before serving, add the mushrooms to the salad bowl.

HOUSE DRESSING

    1 egg, whole
    $^1/_2$ cup vinegar
    1 tablespoon mustard
    3 cups oil
    salt and pepper

In a blender combine the egg, vinegar, mustard, salt and pepper. Drizzle in the oil until well blended.

VEAL SCALLOPS ORLOFF

    12 veal scallops, $^3/_8$ inch thick
    Mushroom Duxelles (recipe below)
    10 ounces Veal Cream Sauce (recipe below)
    4 ounces whipped heavy cream
    2 ounces Hollandaise sauce
    salt and pepper
    flour
    butter

Place the scallops between sheets of waxed paper and pound briefly. Dredge in flour and season with salt and pepper. Place the butter in a skillet over moderately high heat. When the foam subsides arrange 3 or 4 pieces of veal in the skillet. Sauté on one side for 2 to 3 minutes. Remove to a warm platter and continue cooking the rest of the veal.

To assemble, combine Veal Cream Sauce, Hollandaise and whipped cream. Arrange veal on a warm platter, top with Mushroom Duxelles and cover with sauce. Glaze just before serving.
Note: Whenever you add Hollandaise and whipped cream, the sauce cannot come to a boiling point or it will curdle.

MUSHROOM DUXELLES

    1 pound mushrooms, sliced
    3 shallots, peeled
    salt and pepper
    1 tablespoon heavy cream

Purée mushrooms and shallots in a food processor or blender. Season with salt and pepper. Cook over high heat until all moisture has evaporated; the mushrooms will turn dark. Before using, add cream to loosen and lighten the mixture.

VEAL CREAM SAUCE

2 pounds veal bones
3 onions, sliced
4 carrots, sliced
3 stalks celery, sliced
4 ounces butter
4 ounces flour
$1/2$ gallon chicken stock
salt and pepper
1 teaspoon thyme
2 bay leaves
1 cup heavy cream
$1/2$ cup Madeira

In a 425° oven roast veal bones with onions, carrots and celery, until a light color is formed on the bones. Add butter and flour, mixing well. Cook 5 minutes in the oven.

Remove pan from the oven and add chicken stock, salt, pepper, thyme and bay leaves. Simmer over a burner for 2 hours. Strain and adjust seasonings. Add cream and Madeira. Set aside and keep warm.

CHOCOLATE POT DE CRÈME

1 quart half and half
$1/2$ vanilla bean
$1/2$ cup sugar
9 egg yolks
2 whole eggs
$1/4$ pound Baker's semi-sweet chocolate, melted

Heat the half and half with vanilla and sugar in a double boiler over boiling water. Stir until the sugar has dissolved. Beat the egg yolks and eggs together and slowly pour the hot cream over them, stirring vigorously. Add the chocolate and stir quickly until the mixture is blended.

Immediately pour the mixture into crème pots or individual heatproof dishes. Take off any foam. Place the pots in a water bath (make sure the water is hot). Bake at 300°, until a knife inserted in the center comes out clean, or approximately 50 to 60 minutes. Chill until ready to serve.

JOUR ET NUIT

3003 M Street, N.W. · Washington, D.C. · (202) 333-1033

For a relaxing evening in Georgetown go to Jour et Nuit. The building is a beautiful example of Federal architecture and is held in trust as a national historic landmark.

Select from one of three dining rooms. The Terrace offers diners a chance to dine in a garden party ambiance. For more intimate dinner surroundings, the Provençal Room provides a colonial atmosphere by an open fire in winter. Candlelight tables and crystal chandeliers offer another possibility in the Formal Room. In each room you will find the service attentive and personalized.

The menu offers a wide variety of dishes, with special emphasis on seafood. Trout Wellington, the specialty of the house, is a fresh trout served en croute with a bouquetiere of vegetables. It's a beautiful dish, but we found the recipe too complex and demanding for home preparation. The red snapper, a little less intricate to prepare, is just as elegant and distinctive.

The appetizer included here, Pheasant aux Feuilles, is unique. You may want to use it as an entrée when you plan an impressive luncheon. The hazelnut torte you will find addictive and sinfully satisfying. Be prepared for requests for the recipe.

Jour et Nuit

Sandeman Royal Corregidor Sherry	Pheasant aux Feuilles (Pheasant in Puff Pastry)
	Mussel Soup
Meursault Lupecholet 1978	Red Snapper Dugléré
	Endive, Watercress and Mushroom Salad
Château Contet Barsac 1975	Hazelnut Almond Torte

Pheasant in Puff Pastry

(Cornish game hen or breast of chicken may be substituted for the pheasant.)
2 small pheasant
1 cup white wine
2 ribs celery, sliced
3 carrots, diced
1 small onion, diced
2 sprigs parsley
2 bay leaves

In a saucepan combine 2 cups water and the wine, vegetables and herbs and simmer for 15 minutes to combine flavors. Place the pheasant in the pan, cover with buttered wax paper and poach for 25 to 30 minutes or until done. Remove the pheasant from pan, discarding the skin and bones. Shred the meat and set aside. Strain the liquid (hot stock) through cheesecloth or fine sieve and keep warm while preparing the roux.

Roux

$^1/_4$ cup butter

$^1/_4$ cup flour

$1^1/_2$ cups hot stock

$^1/_2$ cup heavy cream

2 tablespoons Madeira

salt and white pepper

2 carrots (julienned)

$^1/_4$ pound mushrooms, sliced

$^1/_2$ small onion, minced

3 artichoke bottoms, thinly sliced (canned or frozen artichokes may be used in lieu of steaming one's own, but there will be some sacrifice in flavor)

To make the roux, melt the butter in a $1^1/_2$ quart saucepan and whisk in the flour until smooth. Cook over a very low flame, stirring constantly, for 5 to 10 minutes or until the roux turns a pale golden brown; it also should acquire a slightly nutty aroma. Cool slightly. In small amounts, whisk the hot stock into the roux, being sure to stir until smooth after each addition. Cook the sauce, stirring frequently, until thick. Simmer for an additional 30 minutes, stirring frequently to prevent scorching. Add the cream, Madeira, salt and pepper to taste. Simmer for 5 more minutes to combine flavors.

Sauté the julienned carrots, diced mushrooms and minced onions in butter until soft. Add the meat and vegetables and chill.

Pastry

$^1/_2$ pound homemade or purchased puff pastry

1 egg, well beaten (egg wash)

flour

Preheat oven to 375°.

On a lightly floured surface, using long and even-pressured strokes in all directions, roll out the puff pastry to a 14 inch by 12 inch by $^1/_8$ inch rectangle. Cut the rectangle in half, lengthwise. The two 14 inch by 6 inch strips of pastry will form the top and bottom of the tart. Spread the chilled pheasant mixture on the center of one strip of pastry leaving at least a $^1/_2$ inch margin on all sides. Brush the margin with the egg wash. Roll the second strip of pastry slightly longer and wider than the first. Lay the pastry strip across the top of the pheasant mixture, pressing down on all sides and notching the edges with the bottom tart.

Using the tines of a fork, mark the edges of the tart, pressing down firmly to anchor the top and bottom layers of pastry together. Brush the top of the tart with the egg wash. Cut 5 small slits, or vents, in the top of the tart to mark your servings and chill for at least $\frac{1}{2}$ hour before baking. Bake in a 375° oven for 30 minutes or until golden brown and well crisped. Allow to set for 5 minutes before slicing and serving.

Mussel Soup

3 dozen mussels
8–10 shallots, diced finely
3 cups white wine
1 cup water
one 16–ounce can tomatoes, crushed
1 sprig parsley, finely chopped
12 ounces butter
$\frac{3}{4}$ cup flour
1 cup heavy cream
$\frac{1}{2}$–1 ounce Pernod
$\frac{1}{2}$ cup salt

Wash mussels in one bath of clean, cold water. Refill the container with cold water and $\frac{1}{2}$ cup salt; let mussels soak for 1 hour. Drain and refill with cold water and let the mussels stand for $\frac{1}{2}$ hour. Clean and beard the mussels.

Place $\frac{1}{2}$ of the shallots and wine and water in a covered pan and bring to the point of steaming. Place the mussels in the pan and steam until just open. Strain the liquid, using cheesecloth. Shell the mussels and discard any that are not open; set the mussels aside.

Place the strained liquid in a saucepan with tomatoes, the remaining shallots and parsley and simmer for $\frac{1}{2}$ hour. Make a roux with the butter and flour, and allow the roux to cook for 15 minutes. (With such small quantities as used here, it is wise to use a double boiler.) Add the liquid to the roux while stirring slowly. Allow the mixture to cook slowly for $\frac{1}{2}$ hour.

When cooked, add cream (after having added a small amount of the hot liquid to the cream first), Pernod, mussels, salt and pepper to taste.

RED SNAPPER DUGLÉRÉ

6–8 ounces of fresh Red Snapper per person

VELOUTÉ (FISH STOCK)

1 pound fish bones (preferably sole)
$1/_2$ onion, diced
2 celery stalks, chopped
2 carrots, chopped
1 cup white wine
3 cups water
3 sprigs parsley
12 ounces butter
$3/_4$ cup flour

Add the fish bones, onion, celery, carrot and parsley to cold water and white wine. Bring to a slight boil and simmer for $1/_2$ hour. Remove from heat and strain the liquid through cheesecloth. Make a roux with butter and flour, using a double boiler, and add the fish stock, stirring constantly until liquid is totally added. Cook for $1/_2$ hour and season with salt and pepper. Extra Velouté may be frozen for later use as a soup base.

HOLLANDAISE

6 egg yolks (save egg whites for torte)
$1^1/_2$ cups clarified butter
3 tablespoons lemon juice
salt and white pepper
Tabasco

Add yolks and lemon juice to a double boiler. Place over heat and whisk the yolks until they begin to thicken. Slowly add the butter in droplets until it is incorporated into the egg mixture. If it becomes too thick, a small amount of warm water may be added. Season with white pepper, salt, and 2 or 3 drops of Tabasco.

CONCASSE

>one 16 ounce can tomatoes, drained and chopped
>$1/2$ onion, chopped
>$1/2$ bay leaf
>$1/2$ cup white wine
>$1/2$ teaspoon thyme
>salt and pepper to taste

Fully drain and chop tomatoes; place in saucepan with onions, white wine, bay leaf and thyme. Cook until the liquid has been reduced. Purée in a blender.

SAUCE

>$1/2$ pint heavy cream

To prepare the Red Snapper, bake in oven at 375° for 5 to 10 minutes in a lightly oiled pan.

Combine the Hollandaise with 1 cup Velouté and add $3/4$ cup Concasse. Enrich the sauce with $1/2$ pint heavy cream, whipped. Cover the fish with sauce and lightly brown under broiler. This dish should be served with boiled potato and fresh vegetable.

ENDIVE, WATERCRESS AND MUSHROOM SALAD

>3 small or 2 large stalks Belgian endive
>1 bunch watercress
>$1/4$ pound fresh mushrooms

Discard any wilted or outer leaves of the endive. Quarter the stalks and cut out the core. If necessary, clean the leaves with a damp cloth. *Do not* immerse the leaves in water. When wet, the semi-bitter taste of fresh endive becomes very bitter.

Wash the watercress, discarding the tough lower stems, and wrap the tender stalks and leaves in a damp paper towel until ready to use. Wash and thinly slice the mushrooms.

When ready to serve, place on each salad plate a bed of watercress topped with a layer of endive leaves and a layer of mushrooms. Top the salad with the vinaigrette dressing and serve immediately.

CREAMY VINAIGRETTE DRESSING

> 2 egg yolks (reserve the whites for use in dessert)
> 3 tablespoons red wine vinegar or fresh lemon juice
> $1/2$ clove garlic, crushed
> 1 teaspoon Dijon mustard
> salt and freshly ground pepper
> $1^1/_2$ cups peanut or safflower oil

In a small bowl, combine the egg yolks, vinegar, garlic and mustard. Slowly add the oil, drop by drop, thoroughly incorporating the oil into the eggs with each addition. A creamy dressing of almost mayonnaise consistency should result. If necessary, thin with additional vinegar or water. Season with salt and pepper.

HAZELNUT ALMOND TORTE

> $1^1/_3$ cups ground almonds (2 cups whole nuts without skins)
> $1^1/_3$ cups ground hazelnuts (2 cups whole nuts without skins)
> 1 cup sugar
> 10 egg whites at room temperature
> 2 tablespoons sugar
> $1/2$ teaspoon vanilla extract
> $1/2$ teaspoon almond extract
> salt
> powdered sugar
> crushed almond slices
> 3 cups desired filling (liqueur flavored whipped cream or chocolate mousse)

Preheat oven to 325°. Line the bottom of a jelly roll pan with wax paper. Butter and flour pan. In a blender or food processor, grind the nuts, a handful at a time, being sure not to grind to a paste. Note that the ground nuts are a flour substitute for this cake. Combine ground nuts with sugar, sieving through fingers to disperse lumps; set aside.

In a clean, *dry* stainless steel or copper bowl, beat the egg whites with a pinch of salt until soft peaks form. Add sugar and extracts and beat until stiff and glossy.

Quickly, but carefully so as not to deflate the meringue, fold in the nut mixture a handful at a time. Turn the meringue into the pan, smoothing and leveling the top as you proceed. The cake will not rise or shift as it bakes. Bake the cake in the middle level of the oven, turning occasionally to assure even cooking. Bake for 30 to 40 minutes or until golden in color and the center springs back to a light touch. While still warm, slice the cake into 3 equal parts and trim any uneven edges. Allow to cool in the pan. When ready to assemble, carefully remove layers from pan and peel off the waxed paper. Spread the bottom two layers with liqueur-flavored, stiffly beaten whipped cream or chocolate mousse. (Be sure to reserve enough filling to spread around the sides of the cake.) Add the top layer and ice the sides of the cake. Press the almond slices into the sides of the cake and coat the top with a thin layer of powdered sugar, sprinkled through a fine sieve. Allow the cake to chill and set for one hour before serving. This cake will keep well for several days under refrigeration, but there is a considerable loss of flavor when frozen.

LA MICHE

7905 Norfolk Avenue · Bethesda, Maryland · (301) 986-0707

La Miche was an exciting discovery. It is located off Wisconsin Avenue in the heart of the business district of Bethesda, Maryland, a highly unlikely place for a French country restaurant. It fulfills all three qualifications one looks for in an excellent restaurant: good food, good service, and a comfortable environment.

Be sure to sample the breads. They are not to be missed!

The memory of La Miche's appetizer, Brochette of Sea Scallops with Green Bean Mousse and Beurre Rouge will cause you to go back again and again. Now it can be made at home. It is a great introduction to any meal. It also would make an elegant luncheon. The colors make this dish a particularly appealing choice for the Christmas season.

La Miche

Mâcon-Viré	Brochette of Sea Scallops Beurre Rouge (Skewered Sea Scallops with Red Butter)
Moulin-à-Vent	Roast Duck au Miel Sauce au Gingembre (Roast Duck in Honey with Ginger Sauce)
	Turnips Tourné (Sautéed Turnips)
Champagne Ayala Brut	Salade de Fruits Exotiques Coulis de Fraise (Exotic Fruit Salad with Strawberry Coulis)

Brochette of Sea Scallops

1 pound sea scallops
1½ teaspoons thyme
2 tablespoons olive oil
juice of 2 limes
salt and pepper to taste

Place scallops on 6 small skewers. In a shallow pan combine thyme, olive oil, lime juice, salt and pepper. Set skewers in marinade and refrigerate for several hours.

Green Bean Mousse

1 pound green beans
salt and pepper
¼ cup heavy cream
4 egg yolks
dash nutmeg

Cook the fresh green beans in boiling salt water for 5 to 10 minutes. Drain and rinse them thoroughly to stop further cooking.

In a blender or food processor combine beans, cream and egg yolks. Season with nutmeg, salt and pepper.

Bake mousse in a buttered soufflé mold set in a pan of boiling water for 20 minutes at 350°. Cover mold with aluminum foil. Remove from oven and keep hot.

BEURRE ROUGE

$^1/_2$ pound shallots, chopped 1 pound butter
4 cups red wine salt and pepper
$^1/_4$ cup heavy cream

In a large frying pan sauté shallots in red wine. Continue cooking until wine is completely reduced. Add the heavy cream and bring to a boil. Add butter in small quantities. Season with salt and pepper. Strain sauce through a fine sieve and keep warm.

To serve, remove scallops from marinade and broil approximately 4 inches from the heat source, turning several times. Place broiled scallops on top of individual servings of mousse. Serve Beurre Rouge in individual cups and garnish with watercress.

ROAST DUCK IN HONEY WITH GINGER SAUCE

3 small ducks
8 ounces honey

SAUCE

10 ounces duck stock (follow any recipe for chicken stock, substituting duck bones)
2 tablespoons honey
2 tablespoons fresh ginger root, chopped
$^1/_2$ teaspoon cornstarch

Brush the ducks with honey and place breasts up in a roasting pan; set in the middle level of a 400° oven to brown lightly for 15 minutes. Reduce heat to 350° and cook for approximately 45 minutes longer.

In a saucepan, over medium heat, combine duck stock, honey and fresh ginger root. Cook for 30 minutes and remove from heat, adding cornstarch mixed with a small amount of water. Strain the sauce through a fine sieve. When ready to serve pour over duck.

The full flavor of turnips goes well with duck and the chef recommends Turnips Tourné as an accompaniment to this meal.

Turnips Tourné

2 pounds turnips
4 ounces butter
sugar and salt

Wash and peel turnips and dice in large cubes. Cook in boiling water to cover until soft, about 30 minutes. Just before serving, sauté in butter with salt and a touch of sugar.

Exotic Fruit Salad with Strawberry Coulis

2 pineapples	1 pound strawberries
4 kiwis	4 tablespoons Grand Marnier
4 mangoes	5 tablespoons sugar
4 papayas	1 pint heavy cream

Cut the pineapples in quarters lengthwise, cutting first in half and then cutting in half again. Remove meat, slice and set aside.

Peel and slice kiwis, mangoes and papayas. Combine with pineapple. Sprinkle one tablespoon sugar and one tablespoon Grand Marnier over fruit and marinate for 10 minutes.

Store the pineapple shells in the freezer until ready to serve. Wash and hull the strawberries. Purée the strawberries in the food processor or blender with 2 tablespoons of sugar and 3 tablespoons of Grand Marnier. Strain the strawberry coulis through a fine sieve and refrigerate.

Pour the cream into a chilled bowl and beat slowly until it forms soft peaks. Fold in 2 tablespoons of sugar and 1 tablespoon of Grand Marnier. To serve, arrange the sliced fruit in the pineapple shells. Spoon cream over the fruit and serve on dessert plates with the strawberry coulis.

LA NIÇOISE

1721 Wisconsin Avenue, N.W. · Washington, D.C. · (202) 965-9300

Entertainment is a significant part of a visit to La Niçoise. The atmosphere is upbeat and fast paced, and service is quick—it should be, the waiters serve the guests on roller skates. If your humor is slap-stick, you will enjoy the weekend floor show.

La Niçoise serves good French food. The menu is extensive and includes a number of daily specials. Because the restaurant serves mainly Mediterranean food, it is not surprising that it chose Salade Niçoise for this book.

The Veal Normandy is cooked in Calvados, a French apple brandy, and served with apples sautéed in butter. This recipe is included in the book and is guaranteed to bring compliments.

LA NIÇOISE

Estandon White

La Soup au Pistou
(Soup with Pesto)

La Salade Niçoise

Estandon Red

Les Côtes de Veau Normande
(Veal Chops Normandy)

Clafoutis aux Cerises
(Cherry Pastry)

SOUP WITH PESTO

1 large carrot, chopped
1 large turnip, peeled and diced
4 ounces navy beans
2 large zucchini, diced
3 potatoes, peeled and diced
3 medium onions, chopped
parsley to taste
3 large tomatoes, peeled and chopped
6 tablespoons olive oil
7 cups hot water
salt and ground pepper to taste
1 cup cooked macaroni ($1/2$ cup uncooked)
3 cloves garlic
6 leaves fresh basil, washed and well dried
1 cup parmesan cheese

In a large soup pot, sauté the vegetables with 3 tablespoons of olive oil over low heat. Reduce by one third. Add hot water and simmer for 45 minutes or until the vegetables are tender. Season with salt and pepper and add the cooked macaroni. If necessary add more water.

In a mortar and pestle, crush the garlic and basil leaves. Add the parmesan cheese and remaining olive oil to this preparation. Set aside. When ready to serve, top with the parmesan cheese mixture.

La Salade Niçoise

2 heads Boston lettuce
1 cucumber, peeled and finely sliced
2 green peppers, cut into thin strips
$^3/_4$ cup ripe olives from Nice
6 spring onions, chopped
10 ounces tuna, drained
12 fillets of anchovies
6 tomatoes, quartered
3 cold hard-boiled eggs, peeled and quartered
6 leaves basil, chopped
1 clove garlic, minced
4 tablespoons olive oil
juice of 2 lemons
salt and pepper

Wash and spin the lettuce dry. Arrange a bed of lettuce on 6 salad plates.

In a small bowl, combine the cucumbers, green peppers, olives and onions. Distribute evenly on the plates. On top of this place the tuna and anchovies. Around the salad, alternate quarters of tomatoes and eggs. Sprinkle with basil and garlic. Whisk the olive oil and lemon juice together and drizzle over the top. Adjust salt and pepper to taste.

Veal Chops Normandy

6 veal chops
flour
2 ounces butter
3 shallots
1 pound fresh mushrooms
3 ounces Calvados
1 pint heavy cream
6 apples, peeled and quartered

Dredge the veal chops with flour. Melt the butter in a heavy iron skillet. Add the chops and brown lightly on both sides. Place skillet in oven and cook, covered, for 15 minutes at 375°. Remove the skillet from the oven and place the veal on a warm platter. Discard any pan drippings and return skillet to burner. Add chopped shallots and sliced mushrooms. Sauté until slightly blonde. Add the Calvados. When reduced to approximately 1 ounce, add the heavy cream. Simmer slowly for 5 minutes.

In a small frying pan sauté apples in butter until al dente. Cover the veal with the sauce and serve with the apples.

CHERRY PASTRY

10 ounces pitted cherries
2 ounces flour
1 ounce butter, melted
1 egg
1 ounce sugar
1 cup milk
1 tablespoon cognac
1 cooked pie shell

Preheat oven to 350°.

Line the bottom of the cooked pie shell with the cherries. In a mixing bowl, beat together the flour, butter, egg and sugar. Add the milk and cognac, blending well. Pour the mixture over cherries and bake at 350° for 35 to 40 minutes, until custard is set. Serve hot and sprinkle with sugar just before serving.

L'AUBERGE CHEZ FRANÇOIS

332 Springvale Road · Great Falls, Virginia · (703) 759-3800

Chez François did something no other restaurant has done. It moved from its downtown location to the rural countryside of Virginia, a more comfortable setting for a French country inn. It continues to serve the best in Alsatian cuisine. Founded by François Haeringer, a native of Alsace, the restaurant is now run by his son, Jacques. Reservations are filled two weeks in advance. Washingtonians obviously have not been deterred by the thirty minute drive.

The Coq au Riesling d'Alsace exemplifies Alsatian cooking. The chicken is marinated in a white wine from the region. The Haeringers have shared this family recipe. It is one of the most delectable dishes from any restaurant, and now it is yours!

L'AUBERGE CHEZ FRANÇOIS

Trimbach Riesling

Marinated Fish Salad

Le Coq au Riesling d'Alsace
(Chicken in Wine)

Broccoli

Île Flottante
(Floating Island)

Marinated Fish Salad

juice of 10 lemons
juice of 2 limes
1 teaspoon fresh minced dill
2 teaspoons crushed coriander
salt and fresh cracked pepper
caviar
2 scallions, minced
2 shallots, minced
6 large mushrooms
1 pound fresh salmon fillets, cut into thin slivers
1 pound fresh sea scallops, sliced to form thin circles
Boston lettuce (enough to cover 6 salad plates)
safflower oil

In a medium-sized bowl add the juices from the lemons and
limes. Season with dill, pepper, coriander, salt and pepper.

Place the salmon and scallops in two separate small bowls.
Cover with the lemon and lime juices and marinate in the refrigerator for at least a couple of hours. (May be made a day ahead.)

To serve this appetizer, form a bed of lettuce on individual
salad plates. Form a circle with the strips of salmon and place
scallops on top. Season with coriander, salt and pepper. Garnish
with caviar and sliced mushrooms. Fresh fruit may be added if in
season. Just before serving, sprinkle with safflower oil.

Chicken in Wine

2 chickens, 2–2^1/$_2$ pounds each
1 bottle Riesling wine
fresh cracked pepper
^{1}/$_2$ teaspoon salt
^{1}/$_2$ teaspoon thyme
2 cloves
1 bay leaf
^{1}/$_2$ onion, sliced
^{1}/$_2$ carrot, sliced

Debone the chickens and reserve the bones for later use. Place chicken parts in a shallow dish with $^1/_2$ bottle of wine. Season with pepper, salt, thyme, cloves, bay leaf, onion and carrot and allow to marinate overnight.

CHICKEN STOCK

> chicken bones
> bay leaf
> $^1/_2$ onion, sliced
> $^1/_2$ carrot, sliced
> pepper
> thyme
> 2 tablespoons butter
> 2 tablespoons flour

In a stockpan, add chicken bones and cover with cold water. Season with above ingredients. Bring to a boil, reduce heat and simmer for about 1 hour, skimming as necessary. Strain, degrease and keep warm.

In a small frying pan, blend the butter and flour together to form a roux. Add the roux to the hot chicken stock and beat with a wire whisk. Simmer for a few minutes. The sauce should be thick enough to coat a spoon lightly. Set sauce aside.

> 1 strip bacon
> $^1/_4$ cup onions, minced
> pinch fresh garlic
> 1 cup wine
> 1 cup marinade (from preceding recipe)
> 1 cup white chicken stock sauce (from preceding recipe)
> 3–4 tablespoons heavy cream

Remove chicken from marinade and set marinade aside for later use. Dry the chicken thoroughly and season with salt and pepper. Sauté bacon in a dutch oven. Add onion and cook very slowly until translucent in color. Add chicken parts and brown in hot fat (350° for 10 minutes) with a pinch of garlic. Remove bacon and cover chicken with equal portions of wine, marinade and stock sauce. Allow to boil for 3 to 5 minutes, reducing the liquid. In the final minute of boiling add heavy cream.

BROCCOLI

2–3 heads broccoli (cut off bottom stems)
1 medium potato, pealed
3–4 scallions, chopped
$\frac{1}{2}$ stick butter
$\frac{1}{4}$ cup heavy cream

Steam broccoli and potato in small amounts of water in two separate pots. Drain both and combine in the top of a double boiler over medium heat. Blend well with butter, onions and cream. Serve in a soufflé dish.

FLOATING ISLAND

2 tablespoons butter
1 tablespoon sugar

MERINGUE

8 egg whites
1 cup sugar
$\frac{1}{3}$ cup golden raisins
Kirsch
1 teaspoon grated lemon
pinch salt
1 teaspoon vanilla

CRÈME ANGLAISE

5 egg yolks
$\frac{1}{2}$ cup sugar
2 cups boiling milk
Kirsch

Caramel Glaze

$\frac{1}{3}$ cup sugar
$\frac{1}{3}$ cup water
kiwi fruit for garnish

Soak raisins in Kirsch overnight. Drain before using.

Preheat oven to 325°. Butter a 2-quart baking dish or charlotte mold ($3\frac{1}{2}$ to 4 inches deep). Sprinkle sugar in the mold, shaking out excess, and set mold aside.

Beat the egg whites until they begin to form soft peaks. Add pinch of salt and gradually add sugar and continue beating until the peaks are firm.

Beat in the vanilla and grated lemon. Remove bowl from beater and gently fold in the raisins. Pour meringue into mold. Bake in a bain marie (water bath) for 35 to 40 minutes at 325°. After baking let cool for 30 minutes, then refrigerate for at least an hour.

In a copper pan, over low heat, beat the yolks and sugar until well blended. Gradually add the boiling milk and continue beating until smooth. Cook over moderate heat until the sauce thickens just enough to coat a spoon. Do not boil. Remove from heat and sprinkle with Kirsch. Chill the custard sauce.

To make caramel, place sugar and $\frac{1}{2}$ of the water in a saucepan and shake pan over moderately high heat until the sugar has dissolved completely. Boil the sugar, shaking pan occasionally until the syrup turns a light brown color (3 to 4 minutes). Add remaining water. Simmer for an additional minute. Use immediately.

To assemble dish, pour custard sauce into a shallow glass bowl. Carefully unmold the island (meringue). Lower onto the custard so it floats. Dribble threads of caramel over the island. Serve chilled, garnished with slices of kiwi fruit.

Le Provençal

1234 20th Street, N.W. · Washington, D.C. · (202) 223-2420

People who go out of their way to find good French food are familiar with Le Provençal. It attracts a clientele not seeking to be seen but rather desiring fine dining, which is exactly what Le Provençal offers.

Jacques Blanc, working chef and owner of Le Provençal, recently was honored by the School of Hotel and Restaurant Administration of Cornell University as their first "Distinguished Visiting Chef."

He specifically chose a meal typical of one served in his native Provence. The veal medallions are prepared with a tomato and cream sauce. Your dinner party guests will talk about this dish for months thereafter! Ours certainly have.

And for die-hard crêpe fans, serve Monsieur Blanc's Apple Crêpes Normande. Flame at the table for oohs and ahs!

Le Provençal

Hermitage Blanc or
Sancerre

Champignons Poivrade
(Mushrooms in Pepper Sauce)

Caesar Salad

Medallions de Veau au Basilic
(Veal with Basil)

Les Crêpes Normande

Mushrooms in Pepper Sauce

$4^1/_2$ tablespoons olive oil
$1^1/_2$ onion, minced
3 cloves garlic
$4^1/_2$ leaves laurel
dash freshly ground pepper
pinch thyme
pinch oregano
pinch coriander
pinch fennel
$^3/_4$ cup dry white wine
$1^1/_2$ pounds mushrooms

In a saucepan, put the olive oil, onion, garlic and seasoning, simmering for a few minutes. Add the white wine and allow it to boil for 2 more minutes. Clean and slice the mushrooms. Add mushrooms and boil rapidly for 4 to 5 minutes. Remove from heat and place in refrigerator. Serve cold as an hors d'oeuvre on lettuce.

Caesar Salad

2 small heads romaine lettuce
2 cloves garlic
6 anchovy fillets
4 teaspoons red wine vinegar
2 tablespoons Dijon mustard
dash salt and pepper
2 eggs (soft-boiled)
1 cup olive oil
croutons
parmesan cheese, grated

Tear the lettuce into small pieces and place in salad bowl. In a separate bowl mash the garlic and anchovy fillets into a fine paste.

Add the vinegar, mustard, salt, pepper and soft-boiled eggs and mix well. Add the olive oil and continue mixing until all the ingredients are well blended. Pour over the lettuce and sprinkle with croutons and cheese.

VEAL WITH BASIL

2 fresh ripe tomatoes
6 veal medallions, 5 ounces each
salt and pepper
flour
butter
Pernod
3 shallots, chopped
$^1/_2$ cup white wine
2 tablespoons veal stock (see note below)
1 pint heavy cream
fresh chopped basil

Peel and seed the tomatoes and dice into small pieces. Season the medallions with salt and pepper and dust with flour. Quickly sauté the medallions in butter until they are brown on both sides. Flame with the Pernod. Remove the veal from the pan and keep warm. To the pan drippings, add the shallots, diced tomatoes, wine and veal stock. Reduce. Add the cream and basil and heat thoroughly. Pour over the veal and serve immediately.
Note: When making a veal stock follow the recipe for a basic stock, substituting veal bones. Before adding veal bones to your stock, boil first in cold water for five minutes to remove scum, which would cloud your stock.

Crêpes Normande

> 5 ounces flour
> 1 ounce sugar
> 1 pint cold milk
> 3 eggs, plus 1 yolk
> 1 ounce butter, melted
> flavoring (rum or vanilla)
> pinch of salt
> 2 large Golden Delicious apples
> butter
> sugar

Combine the flour, sugar, milk, eggs and flavoring. Mix until smooth. Add the melted butter and continue mixing. Strain if there are any flour lumps remaining.

Peel and slice the apples into small pieces. Sauté in a little butter and sugar until they are soft, about 3 or 4 minutes. Paint a hot crêpe pan with a little butter, then add just enough batter to cover the bottom of the pan. Next add a little of the apple filling and spread it around the crêpe. Pour more crêpe batter on top of the apple filling and continue to cook over moderate heat. Flip to the other side.

Sprinkle with sugar or flame with Calvados.

MAISON BLANCHE

1725 F Street, N.W. · Washington, D.C. · (202) 347-0700

A neighbor to the White House, Maison Blanche attracts its share of legislators, foreign dignitaries and celebrities. It offers diners superb French cuisine in a lavish setting of peachy colors and soft velvet chairs.

The service excels. Telephones may be brought to the tables for necessary calls.

Salmon is a luxury with a well-deserved international reputation. Chef Pierre Chambrin has selected Gravlax, salmon marinated in salt, pepper and sugar, as his appetizer. It's a nice beginning to his Caveton au Miel, duck flavored with raspberry vinegar.

In keeping with the nouvelle cuisine, the dessert is a sensational yet surprisingly simple pear sorbet. Sorbets are French sherbets that often are offered in France as palate refreshers before a main course. Here it is the fine compliment to a delightful dinner.

Maison Blanche

Chardonnay "Château St.
Jean" 1979

Gravlax Salmon

Salade M.C.B.

Cabernet Sauvignon Robert
Mondavi 1977

Caneton au Miel
Sauce Aigre-Douce au Vinaigre
de Framboise
(Duckling with Honey and Bitter-
Sweet Sauce with Raspberry Vin-
egar)

Tarte Tatin

Gravlax Salmon (Marinated Salmon)

1 center cut Coho or King salmon ($1\frac{1}{2}$ pounds)
$\frac{1}{4}$ cup salt and $\frac{1}{4}$ cup sugar combined
3 teaspoons cracked white pepper
2 bunches fresh dill, chopped

Scale and debone salmon. Cut into 2 even pieces along the backbone line. Wipe dry with a paper towel. Rub the salmon pieces with some of the salt and sugar mixture. Sprinkle the bottom of an earthenware baking dish with some of the dill and salt-sugar mixture. Place one piece of salmon, skin side down, in the dish and sprinkle generously with some of the dill, crushed peppercorns and additional salt and sugar mixture. Place the second piece of salmon on this, skin side up. Sprinkle with remaining dill and salt and sugar mixture. Put a board and a 4-pound weight on top. Cover with foil and place in the refrigerator at least 48 hours, turning the fish at least twice during that time. The fish will "leach out" in about 5 hours and the fluid should be poured off.

This dish is not cooked. The action of the seasoning gives this a remarkably good flavor. The salmon must be fresh and should be served immediately after marinating. To serve, slice thinly on the diagonal. Top with the sauce below.

SAUCE

> 3 tablespoons oil
> 1 tablespoon red wine vinegar
> 1 teaspoon sugar
> 1 teaspoon salt
> 1 teaspoon pepper
> 1 tablespoon mustard
> 3 tablespoons chopped dill

Combine above ingredients and blend well.

SALADE M.C.B.

> 1 pound mâche (corn lettuce)
> 1 pound celeriac (celery root)
> juice of 1 lemon
> $^1/_2$ pound cooked sliced beets
> salt, pepper, parsley, chives and chervil
> $^1/_2$ cup vinaigrette dressing

Clean, wash and drain the corn lettuce very well. Peel the celeriac and wipe with lemon juice to prevent darkening. Cut into julienne strips. Peel and julienne the beets. Toss all the ingredients together with the salt, pepper, parsley, chives, chervil and a vinaigrette dressing.

DUCKLING WITH HONEY AND BITTER-SWEET SAUCE WITH RASPBERRY VINEGAR

> 6 small ducklings, $2^1/_2$–3 pounds
> salt and pepper
> oil
> 1 jar honey
> 3 ounces raspberry vinegar
> 1 pint duck stock (see below)
> wild rice

Truss the ducklings and season with salt and pepper. Place them in a hot roasting pan with oil. Roast in 350° oven for 40 to 50 minutes, turning them several times. Remove accumulated fat during roasting and baste with honey. Keep warm while making sauce.

Deglaze the casserole in which the ducklings were cooked by adding the raspberry vinegar and the stock. Bring to a boil. Transfer to a sauce pan and reduce heat. Skim off any fats or impurities that rise to the surface. Strain sauce through a fine sieve and adjust seasoning. Sauce may be thickened with arrowroot.

Carve the ducklings and arrange on a platter. Pour sauce over ducks and serve with wild rice.

Duck Stock

Duck stock may be made with the neck, heart, gizzard and lower wings following the same method as for brown stock. For duck sauce, thicken stock with arrowroot.

Tarte Tatin

7 ounces puff dough
$4^1/_4$ ounces butter
$9^1/_2$ ounces sugar
3 pounds apples

On a floured table, roll out the dough less than $^1/_8$-inch thick into a 10-inch diameter. Place the dough on a plate and prick it with a fork. Refrigerate while you peel, core and halve the apples.

In a cast iron dish, melt the butter and sugar on top of the stove. Arrange the apples in the dish closely together. Continue cooking slowly until the sugar begins to caramelize. Put the dish in a preheated 400° oven for 5 minutes, then cover the apples with the rolled puff dough. Bake at 450° for about 20 minutes. Once cooked, turn the dish over on a serving platter.

MONTPELIER ROOM

15th and M Streets, N.W. · Washington, D.C. · (202) 862-1712

The most elegant dining room in Washington is the Montpelier Room in the Madison Hotel. The waiters are polished and stately. A glance commands their attention.

The dining room is colored in royal blues and gold. The ambience is continental—like walking into another world's way of dining. The elegance is not limited to the decor. The kitchen will please your palate with well-prepared French food.

From appetizer to dessert, every detail has been carefully attended to. A simple appetizer of Smoked Trout with Caviar precedes the Rack of Lamb, served with unusual vegetables and delicious homemade breads. A salad flavored with lemon dressing and served with brie cheese and English water crackers follows. The Key Lime Soufflé with Chocolate Macaroons and demitasses complete the evening.

Montpelier Room

Piesporter Goldtröpfchen Riesling	Smoked Trout with Caviar and Sauce Mousseline Russe
Montrachet	Rack of Lamb with Mint Sauce
	Artichoke Bottoms with Lettuce Purée
	Broiled Tomatoes
	Bibb Lettuce, Watercress, Hearts of Palm and Sliced Mushrooms with Lemon Sauce
	Lemon and Broccoli Breads
Dom Perignon, Brut	Brie and Toasted Almonds
	Key Lime Soufflé and Chocolate Macaroons
	Demitasses

Smoked Trout with Caviar and Sauce Mousseline Russe

$^1/_2$ cup Hollandaise
$^1/_2$ cup heavy cream
$^1/_2$ jar red caviar
2 bunches parsley, stems removed
Tabasco sauce
smoked trout (enough for 6 small servings)

In a blender combine Hollandaise sauce, cream, caviar, parsley and Tabasco sauce and mix well. Chill. When ready to serve pour sauce over smoked trout.

Rack of Lamb with Mint Sauce

> 1 rack of lamb (approximately 12 ribs)
> 2 cloves garlic
> salt and pepper
> 2 cups white bread crumbs

Preheat oven to 325°.

Rub meat with garlic cloves and season with salt and pepper. Bake in oven for 25 minutes or until a meat thermometer inserted into the meat registers 170° (for medium-done lamb). Remove from oven, sprinkle with breadcrumbs and cook 10 minutes longer.

Mint Sauce

> 4 bunches fresh mint, chopped
> 4 tablespoons powdered sugar
> 5 ounces vinegar
> salt and white pepper

Combine all ingredients in a mixing bowl and blend well. Chill until ready to serve.

Artichoke Bottoms Stuffed with Lettuce Purée

> 12 large artichokes
> juice of 2 lemons
> salt

Beginning with the base, strip off the outside leaves until you have gone beyond the curve of the heart. Cut off leaves just above the top of the heart and rub with lemon juice. Place in acidulated water as each one is trimmed.

Cook hearts in boiling water with salt and lemon until soft, about 30 minutes. Just before using the hearts remove from liquid and wash under cold water. Remove the choke with a spoon and trim off the remaining leaf ends.

Lettuce Purée

3 tablespoons butter
7 tablespoons flour
1 cup milk, scalded
$\frac{1}{2}$ teaspoon salt
3 cups puréed drained lettuce
3 teaspoons grated onions
$\frac{1}{8}$ teaspoon nutmeg
4 egg yolks
4 egg whites

In a saucepan, melt butter, blend in flour and stir for 3 minutes, without browning. Gradually stir in milk and cook until thick and smooth. Stir in salt, lettuce purée, onions and nutmeg. Allow mixture to cool slightly. Beat egg yolks until light. Add mixture. Let cool. Beat egg whites until stiff but not dry. Fold $\frac{1}{3}$ of the whites into cooled sauce, then fold in the other $\frac{2}{3}$ very lightly. Place in pastry tube and pipe over artichoke bottoms.

Bake in 325° oven until brown, about 30 minutes.

Broiled Tomatoes

3 large tomatoes
1 small pineapple
$\frac{1}{3}$ pound roquefort cheese

Cut tomatoes in half and arrange them in a buttered baking dish, cut side up. Top each tomato with a fresh pineapple ring and a slice of roquefort cheese. Place in broiler until cheese melts.

Salad

2 heads bibb lettuce, washed and dried
2 bunches watercress, washed, dried and stems trimmed
1 can hearts of palm, drained
$\frac{1}{2}$ pound mushrooms, cleaned and sliced

Arrange lettuce, watercress, sliced mushrooms and hearts of palm on individual salad plates. Before serving top with dressing.

LEMON DRESSING

> 1 cup olive oil
> 2 teaspoons salt
> 2 teaspoons dry mustard
> $\frac{1}{4}$ cup fresh lemon juice
> white pepper

Combine all ingredients and add white pepper to taste. The chef suggests serving this salad with brie cheese, baked at 350° until hot and cheese appears melted. Top cheese with toasted almonds and serve with English water crackers.

LEMON BREAD

> $2\frac{1}{2}$ cups sifted flour
> 3 teaspoons baking powder
> 1 teaspoon salt
> $\frac{1}{3}$ cup butter or margarine
> $1\frac{1}{4}$ cup sugar
> 2 tablespoons grated lemon (about 2 lemons)
> 2 eggs
> 1 cup milk
> $\frac{1}{2}$ cup well-chopped nuts
> $\frac{1}{3}$ cup lemon juice

Preheat oven to 325°

Sift together first three ingredients. Cream together butter, 1 cup of sugar and 1 tablespoon of lemon peel. Add eggs 1 at a time. Add dry ingredients. Gradually pour in milk. Stir until smooth. Fold in nuts. Pour into greased and floured 9-inch by 5-inch by 3-inch loaf pan. Bake 60 to 70 minutes.

Before end of baking time, combine lemon juice, remaining $\frac{1}{4}$ cup of sugar and remaining 1 tablespoon of lemon peel. Heat slowly until sugar dissolves. Glaze bread with lemon syrup after removing from oven. Cool, remove from pan onto rack and do not slice for a couple of hours.

BROCCOLI BREAD

(makes 2 loaves)
3 eggs
1 cup oil
2 cups sugar
1 teaspoon salt
3 teaspoons cinnamon
1 teaspoon vanilla
2 cups broccoli, grated
3 cups flour
1 teaspoon soda
1 teaspoon baking powder
$^{1}/_{2}$ cup raisins
1 cup nuts, chopped

Beat the eggs to blend. Add the oil, sugar and flavorings. Beat until the mixture is thick and foamy. Stir in the broccoli. Combine dry ingredients and add to the mixture, blending well. Fold in raisins and nuts.

Divide batter between 2 buttered and floured 9-inch by 5-inch loaf pans. Bake at 350° for 1 hour.

KEY LIME SOUFFLÉ

2 eggs
$^{1}/_{4}$ cup sugar
1 package gelatin
2 tablespoons water
juice of 2 key limes
2 cups heavy cream
2 teaspoons sugar
8 strawberries, sliced
$^{1}/_{2}$ cup shredded chocolate

Beat eggs with sugar until light. Dissolve gelatin in boiling water and lime juice. Combine with egg and sugar mixture. In a separate bowl whip $1^{1}/_{2}$ cups of cream. Gradually fold into egg and sugar mixture. Spoon into a soufflé dish and decorate with remaining $^{1}/_{2}$ cup of cream (whipped) and sliced strawberries. Sprinkle strawberries with sugar and garnish with shredded chocolate. Refrigerate until ready to serve. Serve with Chocolate Macaroons (recipe below).

CHOCOLATE MACAROONS

2 egg whites
$^{3}/_{4}$ cup superfine granulated sugar
3 cups flaked coconut
confectioners' sugar
1 large chocolate bar

Beat egg whites until they form soft peaks. Gradually beat in sugar and fold in flaked coconut. Dust hands with confectioners' sugar and roll small pieces of dough into 1-inch balls.

Bake on a greased cookie sheet in 325° oven for 15 minutes. Remove from oven and set aside to cool.

Break chocolate bar into small pieces. In a small double boiler melt the chocolate, stirring constantly with a wooden spoon. Remove the chocolate from heat, and carefully dip the cooled macaroons in the chocolate bath. Let harden on wax paper.

THE PRIME RIB

2020 K Street, N.W. · Washington, D.C. · (202) 466-8811

Elegant dining is not limited to French restaurants. The Prime Rib, located in the heart of K Street's "Restaurant Row," offers diners fine American cuisine—Filet Mignon, sirloin steak, steak Diane and center cut prime rib.

The owners insist on exacting standards. Their prices are high, but so is the quality. Their excellence extends beyond their beef dishes. Rack of lamb, veal and seafood dishes show the same consistency and quality. Portions are generous.

The Prime Rib is committed to pleasing those who enjoy the good life, and the atmosphere is sophisticated.

For a simple yet elegant meal, follow the chef's suggestion for a crab imperial dinner, beginning with escargots and ending with Strawberries Romanoff.

THE PRIME RIB

Robert Mondavi Fumé
Blanc 1978

Les Escargots
(Snails)

Imperial Crab

Fried Zucchini

Strawberries Romanoff

SNAILS

3 dozen mushroom caps
2 cups chicken stock
2 cups water
$^1/_2$ cup shallots, finely chopped
6 cloves diced garlic
4 tablespoons minced parsley
$1^1/_2$ cups sweet melted butter
$^1/_2$ teaspoon salt
$^1/_4$ teaspoon white pepper
$^1/_4$ teaspoon coriander
1 can snails (36 count)
sourdough French bread

Preheat oven to 500°.

Poach 36 large mushroom caps in 2 cups of boiling chicken stock and 2 cups water for 5 minutes. Drain, cool and reserve.

Sauté in a saucepan over medium heat shallots, garlic and parsley in the melted butter for 4 minutes. Remove from heat and add salt, white pepper and coriander. Allow to cool. Place ingredients in a container and refrigerate to solidify.

Drain snails and rinse well. Place one snail in each mushroom cap and cover with 1 tablespoon butter mixture. Arrange 6 stuffed mushroom caps in individual escargot dishes and bake in 500° oven for 6 minutes. Serve bubbling hot with sourdough French bread.

IMPERIAL CRAB

$1^1/_2$ cups mayonnaise
3 teaspoons minced parsley
3 well-beaten egg yolks
2 tablespoons Dijon mustard
$^1/_4$ teaspoon white pepper
$^1/_4$ teaspoon cumin
1 teaspoon Worcestershire
2 pounds jumbo lump crabmeat

Preheat oven to 375°.

Remove all cartilage from crabmeat. Combine mayonnaise, parsley, egg yolks, mustard, pepper, cumin and Worcestershire sauce in a large mixing bowl. Add crabmeat and mix gently but thoroughly. Mound into six individual fluted baking shells. Bake in moderate oven until hot and bubbly and lightly browned on top (approximately 10 to 15 minutes).

FRIED ZUCCHINI

6 unpeeled zucchini
3 beaten eggs
2 tablespoons water
$^1/_2$ teaspoon salt
$^1/_4$ teaspoon pepper
flour
oil for frying

Slice unpeeled zucchini lengthwise into julienne strips approximately $^3/_8$ inch in thickness. Place zucchini in salted ice water for 5 minutes. Drain and pat dry.

Combine eggs, water, salt and pepper in a shallow dish. Dredge zucchini in egg mixture and then in flour. Fry in deep oil (approximately 350°–375°) until golden brown. Drain on paper towels and arrange on a hot platter. Serve immediately.

STRAWBERRIES ROMANOFF

3 pints fresh California strawberries
$^1/_2$ cup Cointreau
$^1/_2$ cup Kirsch
3 cups Crème Fraîche
6 sprigs fresh mint

Clean and hull the strawberries and marinate in Cointreau and Kirsch mixture for 3 hours, stirring occasionally. Fold in Crème

Fraîche (available in most fine food stores). Spoon into 6 tulip-shaped champagne glasses and garnish with a sprig of fresh mint. Note: If Crème Fraîche is not obtainable, combine $3/4$ cup sour cream and 3 cups heavy cream in a glass bowl. Let stand in a warm place for 24 hours and then chill for 24 hours. Drain off any whey.

RIVE GAUCHE

1312 Wisconsin Avenue, N.W. · Washington, D.C. · (202) 333-6400

The old guard diners of Washington have long preferred the clubby atmosphere of the Rive Gauche in Georgetown. It offers luxurious dining and plush surroundings and was for many years one of the few restaurants of its kind in Washington. It has faced its new competition well.

The French menu includes a number of extravagant and imported fresh foods from Europe.

Be sure not to overlook the daily specials.

The Côte de Veau Maintenon with Sauce Perigueux will be the highlight of your dinner if you follow the chef's menu closely. The veal chops are covered with mushroom duxelles and a rich white sauce, with sauce Perigueux surrounding these. Two very simple vegetables, string beans and red potatoes, accompany this dish.

Nothing is better to complete a satisfying meal than a fresh fruit sherbet. Glace aux Fraises comes highly recommended!

Rive Gauche

Aloxe-Corton 1976

Les Asperges Verte de Californie
Sauce Mousseline
(Asparagus with Sauce Mousse-
line)

La Côte de Veau Maintenon
Sauce Perigueux
(Veal Chops)

Pommes Château
(Potatoes)

Haricots Verts
(String Beans)

Glace aux Fraises
(Strawberry Sherbet)

Asparagus with Sauce Mousseline

6 pounds asparagus

Wash the asparagus and cut off the tough bottom of each stalk. Peel the tougher bottom part off. Place in a large pot of boiling salt water, and boil gently for 6 to 10 minutes. Drain well and serve with the Sauce Mousseline.

Sauce Mousseline

5 egg yolks
1 pound butter, melted

juice of 1 lemon
$1^1/_2$ cups heavy cream

Put the egg yolks in the top part of a double boiler and beat with a wire whisk until smooth and creamy. Dribble in melted butter and continue beating. Slowly add 2 tablespoons of water. Sharpen Hollandaise with the juice of half a lemon. Continue to mix for one minute. The sauce should be thickened. Pour into a sauce tureen and top with whipped cream (see below).

WHIPPED CREAM

In a chilled metal bowl, beat the heavy cream just until soft peaks form.
Note: Set aside 2 tablespoons of Hollandaise and 2 tablespoons of heavy cream for Veal Chops.

VEAL CHOPS

6 veal chops
salt and pepper
flour
4 ounces butter, softened
1 cup Madeira
6 ounces brown stock
1 ounce truffles, chopped
1 bunch watercress for garnish

Season veal chops with salt and pepper. Dredge in flour and sauté in 2 ounces of butter. Cook slowly over low heat for 3 to 4 minutes on each side. Discard cooking grease and pour in the Madeira. Boil for 5 minutes. Add the brown stock and cook for an additional 10 minutes. Remove the chops to a hot platter. Strain the sauce and add the chopped truffles. Beat the remaining butter into the sauce. Set sauce perigueux aside for final preparation.

MUSHROOM DUXELLES

1 pound mushrooms
$^1/_2$ onion, chopped
1 shallot, chopped
butter
salt and pepper
2 ounces heavy cream

Thoroughly clean and trim mushrooms. Chop them finely. In a frying pan, sauté $^1/_2$ onion and 1 shallot in butter until lightly browned. Add the mushrooms, salt, pepper and cream. Continue to cook over low heat, stirring occasionally until all the moisture has evaporated, about 20 minutes.

WHITE SAUCE

> 1 tablespoon butter
> 1½ tablespoon flour
> 2 cups boiling milk
> 2 tablespoons Hollandaise sauce
> 2 tablespoons whipped cream

Melt the butter in a heavy-bottomed saucepan. Stir in the flour, blending well for 2 minutes. Do not let the sauce brown. Add boiling milk and continue to stir as the sauce thickens. Remove from heat and add the Hollandaise sauce and whipped cream.

When ready to serve, arrange veal chops on an oven proof platter. Top each chop with duxelles, forming a dome. Cover with white sauce and glaze in the oven. Pour sauce perigueux around the chops and garnish with watercress. Serve with Pommes Château and Haricots Verts (recipes below).

RED POTATOES

> 18 red potatoes
> 2 ounces butter
> salt

Wash and peel the potatoes. Cut into the shape of large olives. Melt the butter in a large skillet. Add the potatoes and sauté over low heat, stirring occasionally. Season with salt and continue cooking until the potatoes acquire a fine golden color.

STRING BEANS

> 3 pounds string beans
> 2 ounces butter
> salt and pepper

Wash the beans and remove the ends. Drop beans into boiling salt water and boil them gently for 6 to 8 minutes. Drain the beans and rinse them in cold water to stop the cooking. Just before serving reheat them in butter and season to taste.

STRAWBERRY SHERBET

    2 pounds strawberries
    1 pound sugar
    juice of 1 lemon
    juice of 2 oranges
    1 cup spring water

In a blender or food processor, combine strawberries, sugar, lemon juice, orange juice and spring water. Beat until well blended. Freeze in a stainless bowl until almost set. Remove from freezer and beat again. Return to freezer. Just before serving, place in refrigerator for 15 minutes.

SANS SOUCI

726 17th Street, N.W. · Washington, D.C. · (202) 298-7424

Every city has a restaurant that is a favorite of celebrities. In Washington, Sans Souci has been the spot where visiting celebrities gather for drinks and dinner. At noon the tables are usually occupied by politicians and members of the current administration. It is a place where power dwells.

Dining at Sans Souci is very French. The menu is intentionally limited. Sauces are exquisitely prepared, as one would expect.

The chef shared with us his recipe for red snapper—a colorful Gulf Coast fish. It is served with a white wine cream sauce and a simple fresh vegetable, asparagus.

For a dramatic ending to the meal he suggests a liqueur flavored soufflé: Soufflé Grand Marnier.

SANS SOUCI

Pouilly-Fuissé 1974 or 1976   Marinated Mushrooms

Red Snapper Sans Souci

Asparagus

Soufflé Grand Marnier

Marinated Mushrooms

$1\frac{1}{2}$ pounds mushrooms, cleaned and quartered
3 teaspoons tomato paste
3 cups white wine
dash of coriander, thyme and laurel
salt and pepper

In a frying pan simmer mushrooms in white wine and tomato paste. Season with coriander, thyme, laurel, salt and pepper. Remove pan from heat after 5 minutes. When cool refrigerate. Serve on a bed of lettuce.

Red Snapper Sans Souci

fresh seaweed
3 pounds red snapper, skinned and boned
salt and pepper
1 cup dry white wine
4 tablespoons shallots, chopped
2 cups Crème Fraîche
$1\frac{1}{2}$ cups butter

Preheat oven to 350°.

Layer an oiled sheet of aluminum foil with seaweed. Top with a portion of snapper seasoned with salt and pepper. Cover with a second sheet of aluminum foil. Fold foil to make a papillote (envelope). Place on a rack over a pan of hot water. Bake in oven for 20 to 25 minutes.

In a saucepan, combine the white wine, shallots and Crème Fraîche. Let this mixture simmer over low heat until reduced by three quarters. Whisk in the butter a little at a time. Season with salt and pepper. Keep warm until snapper has finished baking.

When snapper is done, discard the seaweed. Pour the sauce over the fish and serve immediately.

Asparagus

4–6 bundles asparagus spears
3 tablespoons salt
7–8 quarts water

Peel tough outer flesh from asparagus. Tie the asparagus in small bundles and plunge into an oval casserole or wide pan of rapidly boiling salted water. The asparagus should be horizontal. Bring water to a boil again as quickly as possible. When boil is reached, reduce heat and cook 12 to 15 minutes longer, uncovered. Serve immediately with butter.

Soufflé Grand Marnier

1 cup butter
$^1/_2$ cup flour
1 cup sugar
3 cups milk
$^1/_2$ cup Grand Marnier
6 eggs, separated

Butter an eight cup soufflé mold and sprinkle with sugar. Set aside. Preheat oven to 400°.

Melt butter in saucepan. Beat in flour and sugar. Gradually add milk, beating well. Stir over moderately high heat until mixture thickens and comes to a boil. Boil, stirring for $^1/_2$ minute. Sauce will be very thick. Remove from heat and beat for 2 minutes.

Add the 6 egg yolks one at a time, beating the yolks into the sauce with a wire whisk. Set aside to cool.

Beat egg whites with a pinch of salt until soft peaks form. Delicately fold the egg whites into the cool yolk mixture. Add Grand Marnier. Turn the soufflé mixture into the prepared mold, allowing at least $1^1/_2$ inch at the top of the mold for soufflé to rise. Turn oven down to 375° and place mold on the middle level. Bake for 40 to 45 minutes. The top of the soufflé will be golden brown.

1789

1226 36th Street, N.W. · Washington, D.C. · (202) 965-1789

The 1789 was one of Washington's first French continental restaurants of importance. In a city where restaurants come and go, it has maintained its reputation of excellence. The name commemorates the year President George Washington was inaugurated and the village of Georgetown was incorporated.

The restaurant is a handsome house of Federal decor. A brick and cobblestone entrance hall leads to several dining rooms. The Carroll Room, the most formal, houses a collection of prints of the Federal City.

Located downstairs, below the 1789, is the Tombs, a well-known rathskeller. Adjacent to the 1789 is owner Richard McCooey's latest addition, F. Scott's, where diners may complete their evening with after-dinner drinks and dancing.

1789's menu offers a wide variety of seafood hors d'oeuvres; among them are cherrystones on the half shell, herring in sour cream, clams baked in garlic butter, oysters on the half shell and mussels sautéed in shallots and chablis. The soups are rich and full-bodied. The entrée selection is marked by unusual items: broiled quail, reindeer with lingonberries, frog legs in garlic butter.

Your 1789 menu, planned by the chef, includes one of these distinct dishes, domestic rabbit sautéed in a variety of peppercorns. It is rich and uncommonly different.

1789

Beaujolais Villages (red) or
Chardonnay, Trefethen
Vineyard, Napa Valley
(white)

Salade Paradis Vinaigrette
(Paradise Salad)

Soupe aux Moules
(Mussel Soup)

Sauté de Lapin aux Poires Divers
(Rabbit with Peppercorns)

Fraises Grand Marnier
(Strawberries in Grand Marnier)

PARADISE SALAD

1 head romaine lettuce
2 heads escarole
5 ounces mushrooms, cleaned and sliced thin
4 tomatoes, cut into wedges
6 ounces hearts of palm, sliced lengthwise
2 avocados, pitted, peeled and sliced lengthwise

Break the lettuce into pieces and arrange the remaining ingredients artfully on top. Serve with vinaigrette dressing.

VINAIGRETTE DRESSING

3 ounces Dijon mustard
6 ounces red wine vinegar
salt and freshly ground pepper
12 ounces vegetable oil

In a small glass bowl, continuously beat the mustard, vinegar, salt and pepper. Drizzle the oil into this mixture, a little at a time, while beating until emulsified.

Mussel Soup

2$\frac{1}{2}$ pounds fresh mussels
4 ounces butter
$\frac{1}{2}$ ounce shallots, chopped
2 fluid ounces chablis
1 quart heavy cream
2 small tomatoes, peeled, seeded and finely chopped
salt
3 tablespoons parsley

Thoroughly clean mussels in several changes of water. Scrape off beards and rinse well. In skillet sauté the shallots in butter over moderate heat. Add mussels, 2 tablespoons parsley, tomatoes, chablis and cream. Bring to a boil over high heat. Season with salt.

Cover and steam the mussels over reduced heat for 5 minutes or until shells open. Serve garnished with a touch of parsley.
Note: To serve properly, provide soup spoons and cocktail forks, with a little plate for discarding mussel shells.

Rabbit with Peppercorns

2 rabbits, fully dressed (weight should total 5 pounds)
4 ounces olive oil
$\frac{1}{2}$ gallon chablis
1 quart heavy cream
1 ounce crushed mixed peppercorns
3 bay leaves
1$\frac{1}{2}$ teaspoons thyme leaves
salt and fresh black pepper
$\frac{1}{4}$ cup parsley, chopped

Cut rabbits into serving pieces. Sprinkle with salt, pepper and thyme. In a large skillet brown rabbits over high heat in the oil. Transfer rabbits to a large casserole and add chablis, cream, bay leaves and peppercorns. Bring to a boil and reduce liquid to one half. Simmer, covered, over moderate heat for 1 hour and 20 minutes (or until tender). Remove bay leaves. Divide onto 6 heated plates and top with sprinkles of parsley.

Serve with buttered bread, sprinkled with parsley.

Strawberries in Grand Marnier

2 pounds fresh strawberries, stemmed
1 cup superfine granulated sugar
12 ounces Grand Marnier
six 3-ounce scoops vanilla ice cream

Marinate half the strawberries in $^1/_2$ cup sugar and 6 ounces of Grand Marnier. Chill 1 hour.

In a food processor fitted with a steel blade, purée the remaining strawberries, sugar and Grand Marnier.

Place a scoop of ice cream in each of 6 stemmed dessert glasses. Divide marinated strawberries among them and top off with purée.

Tandoor

3316 M Street, N.W. · Washington, D.C. · (202) 333-3376

Tandoor, located in the heart of Georgetown on M Street, offers Washington diners something different: good Indian food in a contemporary setting.

Spices first came from India. The cooking clearly reflects this, for almost all dishes are spiced. The spices can be hot or mild. The waiters at Tandoor, all of them knowledgeable and helpful, can advise you of the most highly spiced dishes and of the milder seasoned dishes. By all means, seek their advice.

The dinner planned for this book begins with Muligatawny Soup, a highly seasoned vegetable soup. Vegetable soups tend to be boring and dull, but this one is not.

The chef suggests serving the Chicken Bara with either rice or parathas (a fried wheat bread). Traditionally, some type of grain is served at all meals.

The Gulab Jamun is an Indian dessert flavored with rosewater and is a nice conclusion to this meal.

Tandoor

Chenin Blanc, San Joaquin Valley

Muligatawny Soup

Chicken Bara

Gulab Jamun

Muligatawny Soup

4 tablespoons white lentils
2 celery stalks, chopped
8 garlic cloves, crushed
2 medium onions, chopped
1 teaspoon fennel seeds, fried
2 large carrots, peeled and diced
2 teaspoons vinegar
2 cinnamon sticks
8 cloves
2 tomatoes, peeled and chopped
2 teaspoons coriander powder
3 teaspoons salt
2 teaspoons ginger
10 peppercorns
3 cups vegetable stock
2 cups hot water
juice of 1 lemon
6 teaspoons chopped onions
1 stick butter
4 tablespoons cooked rice
4 lemons, sliced

Put the lentils, garlic, 2 chopped onions, fennel seeds, carrots, vinegar, cinnamon, cloves, tomatoes, coriander powder and salt in a large pot with the vegetable stock. Bring to a boil, reduce heat and simmer until vegetables are tender, about 30 minutes. Add the water and cook over low heat for 10 minutes. The lentils should be soft. Add lemon juice.

In a separate pan sauté 6 teaspoons chopped onions in butter until onions are light brown. Add to the soup. Spoon 2 teaspoons of cooked rice into each bowl as you serve the soup. Top with a thin slice of lemon.

CHICKEN BARA

2 medium chickens
4 red chili peppers
6 green chili peppers
1 ginger stick, 2 inches long
6 cardamons
1 teaspoon cumin seed
$^1/_2$ coconut, grated
5 garlic cloves
$1^1/_2$ sticks butter
2 onions, chopped
$^1/_2$ cup hot water
6 bay leaves
1 cup coconut milk
4 tablespoons sour cream
pinch saffron
$1^1/_2$ teaspoons salt

Cut the chicken into medium-sized pieces. Wash the chicken pieces and wipe dry, setting aside. In a food processor grind the red chilies, green chilies, ginger, cardamons, cumin seed, coconut and garlic into a fine paste. In a large frying pan melt the butter and sauté the onions until brown. Add the fine paste and stir for 5 minutes. Add the chicken pieces to the pan along with the bay leaves and hot water. Cook for 20 to 25 minutes. Remove bay leaves. Add the coconut milk, sour cream and saffron. Cover with a lid and simmer for 5 minutes. Serve with hot rice or parathas (wheat bread layered with butter, then fried).

GULAB JAMUN

4 cups non-fat dry milk
2 cups self-rising flour
3 tablespoons vegetable oil
$1\frac{1}{2}$ cups milk
5 cups vegetable oil for frying
$\frac{1}{2}$ pound sugar
2 cups water
4 cardamons, crushed
1 teaspoon rosewater

In a large bowl combine dry milk, flour and 3 tablespoons oil. Blend the ingredients together with a fork. Add the milk. At this point the dough will be fairly hard. In a deep fat fryer, heat 5 cups oil to 360° to 375°.

Make a syrup by boiling in a saucepan the sugar and water. Add the cardamons and rosewater.

Form the dough into small balls the size of golf balls. Fry in the hot oil until golden brown. Immerse in the warm syrup. They should be served warm.

TAVERNA CRETEKOU

818 King Street · Alexandria, Virginia · (703) 548-8688

Historic Old Town Alexandria may be an unlikely place to find a classic Greek island taverna. Stroll down King Street to 1818 and discover Taverna Cretekou.

You will dine in Mediterranean-styled rooms with whitewashed walls and curved archways. A garden resembling a Greek courtyard is open for outdoor dining Spring through Fall.

Greeks enjoy dining and always make it a festive occasion. Lively Greek music and spirited waiters make dining at Taverna Cretekou no exception.

The menu is Greek with a number of intriguing appetizers and entrées. Eggplant, stuffed grape leaves and spinach and cheese pies are not to be missed.

For a Greek evening at home begin with a cold appetizer of eggplant and tomatoes followed by Arnipsito, roast leg of lamb cooked in garlic, and of course the Greek salad of greens, tomatoes, olives and feta cheese.

The dessert, Rizogalo, bears no resemblance to cafeteria style rice pudding. It is flavored with the grated rinds and juices of fresh lemons and oranges.

Taverna Cretekou

Castel Danielis

Melizanosalata
(Taverna Appetizer)

Taverna Salad

Arnipsito
(Roast Leg of Lamb)

Rizogalo
(Taverna Pudding)

Taverna Appetizer

1 large eggplant
1 garlic clove, mashed
1 medium onion, finely chopped
1 tablespoon chopped parsley
1 large tomato, peeled and chopped
1 teaspoon marjoram
1 teaspoon of fine herbs (thyme, oregano, sage, rosemary
and basil)
olive oil

Preheat oven to 350°.

Pierce the eggplant with a fork in several places. Place in a baking dish and bake for 50 to 60 minutes. Remove from oven and when cool, peel and chop. In a mixing bowl combine eggplant, garlic, onions, parsley, tomato and herbs. Add enough oil to moisten the mixture. Chill and serve on lettuce with tomato wedges and olives.

Taverna Salad

2 bunches chicory
2 small heads romaine lettuce
4 tomatoes, cut in wedges
2 cucumbers, peeled and sliced
6 spring onions, thinly sliced
12 anchovies
12 Greek olives
capers
$^{1}/_{2}$ pound feta cheese, cut into cubes

Mix all ingredients together in a large salad bowl. Add dressing and serve immediately.

Greek Dressing

$^{2}/_{3}$ cup olive oil
4–6 tablespoons vinegar
oregano
fresh mint, chopped
salt and pepper

Blend oil and vinegar together. Add seasonings.

Roast Leg of Lamb

1 leg of lamb, 5–6 pounds
salt and pepper
3 garlic cloves, slivered
juice of 1 lemon
1 cup white wine
$^{1}/_{2}$ cup olive oil
$^{1}/_{2}$ cup white wine
$^{1}/_{2}$ cup butter, melted
18 small potatoes, peeled
1 tablespoon oregano
$1^{1}/_{2}$ teaspoons thyme

Wash and dry the lamb. Season with salt and pepper. With a knife make small slits in the lamb and insert the slivered garlic. Sprinkle with lemon juice. Pour one cup of wine and $^{1}/_{2}$ cup olive oil over the lamb. Turn the leg to coat it completely with the juices. Marinate for several hours.

Roast lamb in preheated 350° oven for 2 hours. Baste frequently with mixture of $^{1}/_{2}$ cup wine and melted butter. As liquid evaporates add hot water to pan juices and continue to baste. One hour before the roast is done, add potatoes. Season them with salt, pepper and oregano. Baste and turn them during baking.

TAVERNA PUDDING

$^{1}/_{3}$ cup rice
pinch salt
1 quart milk
4 egg yolks
$^{3}/_{4}$ cup sugar
grated rind and juice of 1 orange
grated rind and juice of 1 lemon
1 teaspoon vanilla extract
cinnamon
$^{1}/_{2}$ pint heavy cream

Parboil rice in $^{1}/_{2}$ cup water with a pinch of salt for 5 minutes. Drain. Scald the milk and add drained rice. Cook over low heat, stirring occasionally for 45 minutes.

Beat egg yolks with the sugar. Remove the rice mixture from the heat and slowly stir in the egg yolks, mixing well. Add juices and rinds of orange and lemon. Return to low heat and stir constantly until thick and creamy. Add vanilla and mix well. Pour into sherbet glasses or dessert bowls. Sprinkle with cinnamon and chill. This may be served with whipped cream.

TIBERIO

1915 K Street, N.W. · Washington, D.C. · (202) 452-1915

Tiberio is a formal Italian restaurant. You won't find tables covered with checked tablecloths or candles dripping over wine bottles. Instead you will find waiters in black tie and tables draped in linen.

The pasta is light and cooked to perfection. It is worth sampling either as an appetizer or entrée.

Veal is considered one of the restaurant's specialties, but the chef suggested we include his recipe for steak in this book. The appetizer included here, Mozzarella alla Lucania, is a perfect example of a simple fresh flavor, not marred by a lot of ingredients.

The steak, Francosta di Manzo alla Siciliana, is a striking dish with strong colors—red peppers, black olives and bright red tomatoes—cooked with the steak to enhance the flavor.

Zuppa Inglese is a dessert similar to English Trifle. Rumor has it that the British tourists introduced this dessert to the Italians. The Italians named it Zuppa Inglese since it reminded them of their soup (zuppa). Regardless of its origin, Tiberio's version of this dessert is unequaled.

TIBERIO

Orvieto Seceo Ruffino	Mozzarella alla Lucania (Mozzarella Triangles)
	Spinaci e Funghi (Spinach Salad with Mushrooms)
Corvo	Fracosta di Manzo alla Siciliana (Sirloin Steak Sicilian Style)
	Melanzane al Funghetto (Eggplant)
Picolit	Zuppa Inglese

MOZZARELLA TRIANGLES

> 1 pound mozzarella
> 6 slices white bread (pullman loaf)
> milk
> flour
> 2 eggs, beaten
> bread crumbs
> 3 anchovy fillets
> garlic butter sauce (2 cloves garlic, crushed, and 4 ounces butter, melted)

Cut mozzarella into 6 equal slices, then diagonally to obtain 12 triangles. Remove crust from bread and cut bread into the same size and shape as mozzarella triangles.

Arrange 3 separate bowls for milk, flour and eggs. Dip mozzarella triangles into milk, flour and eggs. Dip the bread triangles into eggs only. Place mozzarella and bread triangles together and roll them in bread crumbs. Fry in a deep fryer at 375° until golden brown. To serve, top with anchovy fillets and brush with garlic butter sauce.

Spinach Salad with Mushrooms

$1/4$ cup vinegar
1 tablespoon mustard
salt and pepper
$1/2$ cup olive oil
2 pounds of spinach
$1/2$ pound mushrooms, sliced

In a small bowl mix the vinegar and seasoning. Slowly whisk in the oil. Blend well.

Clean spinach and discard stems. Arrange on salad plates and top with mushrooms. Drizzle dressing on top.

Sirloin Steak Sicilian Style

2 tablespoons butter
1 medium onion, sliced
3 red bell peppers, sliced
8 ounces mushrooms, quartered
3 tomatoes, peeled and diced with seeds removed
18 black olives, cut in half
oregano
six 12-ounce sirloin steaks (or any size desired)
2 cloves garlic, chopped
salt

Sauté the onions and peppers together in butter. Add mushrooms, tomatoes and olives. Season with oregano and simmer for a few minutes. In a separate pan cook steaks until done as desired. Remove them to a warm platter. Sauté garlic in pan drippings until golden brown. Add the vegetable mixture (onions, peppers, mushrooms, tomatoes and olives) to the garlic. Season with salt. Pour sauce over the steaks and serve immediately.

EGGPLANT

olive oil
3 cloves garlic, chopped
10 baby eggplants, cubed
7-ounce can peeled tomatoes, drained and chopped
fresh basil, chopped
salt and pepper

Heat olive oil in frying pan. Add garlic and sauté. When golden brown add eggplants and sauté briefly. Add tomatoes, basil, salt and pepper. Remove from heat and keep warm for serving.

ZUPPA INGLESE

12-ounce sponge cake or 1 Genoese cake (recipe below)
2 cups prepared vanilla pudding (recipe below)
1 tablespoon chopped candied filling
Amaretto liqueur
cherry pie filling
3 egg whites
6 tablespoons sugar

Slice Genoese or sponge cake into pieces $1/2$ inch thick. Combine pudding and candied fruit in a small bowl. In an ovenware dish about 8 inches in diameter place half of the sponge cake. Sprinkle with Amaretto. Cover with a layer of cherry pie filling and a layer of pudding mixed with candied fruit. Add remaining sponge cake and again sprinkle with liqueur.

Beat egg whites until stiff. Gradually beat in sugar, 1 tablespoon at a time, until egg whites are stiff and glossy. Cover cake with egg whites and bake at 450° until meringue is pale brown.

Vanilla Pudding

$^1\!/_3$ cup cornstarch
$^1\!/_3$ cup sugar
2 cups milk
2 tablespoons vanilla

In a saucepan combine cornstarch, sugar and milk. Stir over low heat until thick. Add vanilla and blend well. Remove and cool.

Genoese Cake

$^3\!/_4$ cup sugar
6 eggs
$1^1\!/_2$ cups self-rising cake flour, sifted
6 tablespoons butter, melted

Preheat oven to 350°.

Place sugar and eggs in top of double boiler. Water in the bottom of the double boiler should be hot but not boiling. Beat until mixture is lukewarm and about twice the original volume. Add butter and stir until well blended. Remove from heat and continue to beat until mixture has cooled completely. Gradually fold in cake flour. Transfer batter into a buttered and lightly floured spring form pan. Bake for 30 to 35 minutes. Cool before cutting.

About the Authors

SHEILA GEOGHEGAN—she's the short one—is a native Washingtonian who has spent all her adult life in the capital area, most of it eating and cooking. When she hasn't been dining out or dining in, she's been variously engaged in public relations, advertising, personnel work and sales. Most recently she's served as right hand, left hand, and glad hand for conservative columnist James J. Kilpatrick. Headwaiters love her. So do her dinner party guests.

BONNIE FITZPATRICK—she's the tall one—came to Washington by way of New York and Pennsylvania, bringing with her a B.A. in psychology and an M.Ed. in guidance and counseling. Currently she is director of guidance at Walter Johnson High School. She's also involved in real estate, photography, skiing and the social whirl; but her chief avocation is gourmet cooking—an art she continues to study at L'Academie Cuisine and other French schools.